SELF-HEALING WITH QIGONG
FOR
LOWER BACK

Regain Back Strength, Stability, and Ease of Movement

Camilo Sanchez, L. Ac, MAOM

Copyright 2019 Camilo Sanchez

Photography by Bethany Otten - www.bethanyotten.com

Thank you for purchasing this E-book. This E-book remains the copyrighted property of the author, and may not be redistributed to others for commercial or non-commercial purposes. If you like to share this E-book with another person, please purchase an additional copy for each recipient. If you are reading this book and did not purchased it, or it was not purchased for your use only, then please return to your favorite E-book retailer and purchase your own copy. Thank you for your support.

Table of Contents

Disclaimer

Section 1 – General considerations

Section 2 – The lower back in Oriental medicine and Qigong

Section 3 – Energy channels and energy centers

Section 4 – Muscle channels

Section 5 – The mind-body connection

Section 6 – Main causes of lower back pain

Section 7 – Life style recommendations

Section 8 – Notes on practicing the exercises

Section 9 – Description of the exercises

About the author

Other titles by Camilo Sanchez

Connect with Camilo Sanchez

Disclaimer

The information provided in this book is written solely for educational and recreational purposes. The author and publishers of this book are not liable or responsible whatsoever for any liability, loss, damage, or injury resulting directly or indirectly from following the instructions, practices, advices, or performances presented in this book. The activities and exercises presented in this book may be too strenuous, difficult, or risky for some people and not suitable for everyone. As with any physical exercise, there is always the risk of injury. Before engaging in this or any exercise program or physical activity it is recommended that you consult with your doctor or primary health provider. Other special cautions may apply to individuals with specific health issues. The advice and information provided in this book is not intended to diagnose, treat, cure, or prevent any disease or medical condition or as a substitute for professional medical care. Please, always use caution when engaging in any exercise program.

Section 1 – General considerations

The lower back sits on the core of the body and it serves as the pillar for proper structure, support, stability, strength, and movement of the whole body.

Due to its central location the lower back area takes a great percentage of the weight of the body. The compressive force of the upper body is transferred down to the lower back region and lower spine. In particular, the fifth lumbar and first sacral vertebras take a great amount of mechanical pressure. In addition, the pull of the gravitational force increases the compressive downward stress upon the body. For this reason, the area of the lower back is easily prone to injury and strain.

The structure of the lower back is comprised of five lumbar vertebras, five sacral vertebras that are fused together at the sacrum, the hips (iliac bone), the coccyx (tail bone), and their supporting soft connective tissues. The lower back vertebras and lower spine are kept in place and properly aligned by ligaments, muscles, and fascia located on either side of the spine. As a result, most structural problems of the lower back area can be traced back to imbalances and disorders of its supporting tissues, which help keep the lumbar structure in place.

At the same time, the lower back area is in close proximity to the sacrum, hips, abdomen, and pelvic regions. As such, disorders of these areas also can affect the structural integrity of the lower back.

VERTEBRAL COLUMN

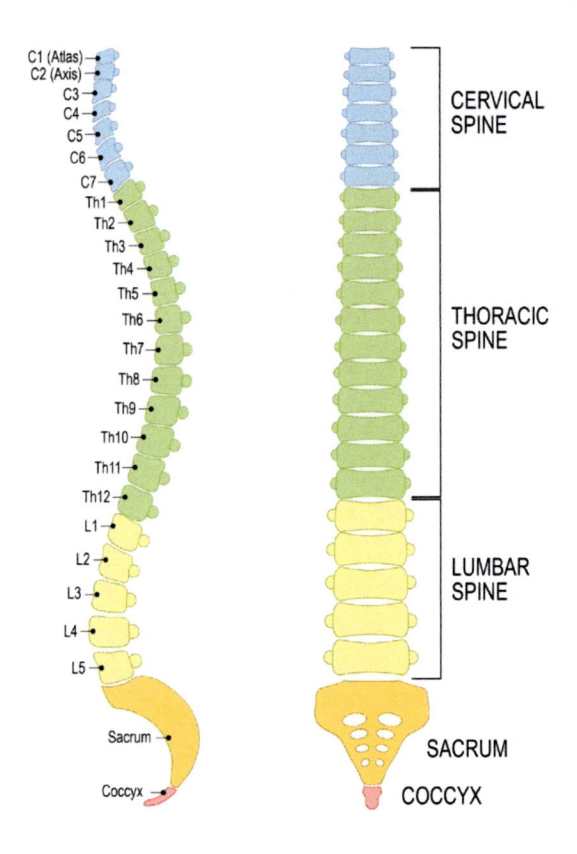

Fig. 1 – The spine: central pillar of the body

Section 2 - The lower back in Oriental medicine and Qigong

In Chinese medicine and Qigong, the lower back area is regarded as "the residence of the kidneys". It is considered that the kidneys also include the functions of the urinary bladder, adrenal glands, and the sex glands or gonads (ovaries in females and testis in males). Accordingly, in Chinese medicine the kidney energy system comprises the urinary, reproductive, and hormonal systems.

At the same time, the kidneys are the source of the original energy of the body (prenatal chi). The prenatal chi determines our inborn nature, inherited traits, constitutional strengths, susceptibility to disease, and basic life force. As such, the lower back area harbors the deep energy of the body and mind responsible for our inner power, courage, sustained effort, and stamina.

Within the five elements model of Chinese medicine, the area of the lower back belongs to the domain of the water element (kidneys and urinary bladder) and it is associated with the core energy of the body.

The elemental energy of water represents the origin of life. It is estimated that life, as we know it, originated from single-celled organisms that developed in a primitive fluid environment. The presence of water is a prerequisite for the emergence of life.

Fig. 2 – Water molecule

Similarly, in the human body, the gestation of a new life takes place within the amniotic fluid of the mother's placenta. Every one of the body's trillions of cells is bathed by the medium of the interstitial fluid circulating outside the cells. Even after birth, and throughout our lives, we still carry the same primitive fluid environment in the plasma of our blood, which has retained the precise saline composition as the marine fluid from where it initially originated.

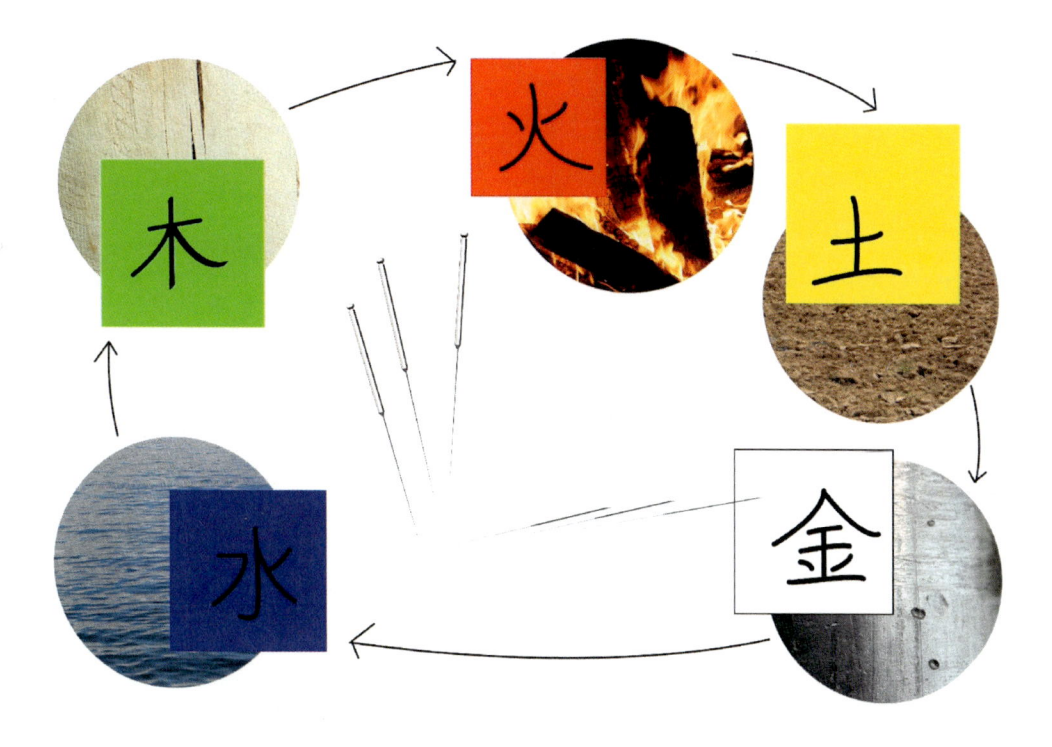

Fig. 3 – The Five Elements of Chinese medicine

Section 3 – Energy channels and energy centers

There are four main acupuncture channels that run along the lower back area as follows.

1. The urinary bladder channel - It has two branches that run 1.5- and 3.0-inches lateral along both sides of the spine.

2. The governing vessel – It travels along the midline of the back.

3. The gall bladder channel – It travels through the buttock and hip areas.

4. The kidney channel – It has an internal branch that connects to the kidneys on the lower back.

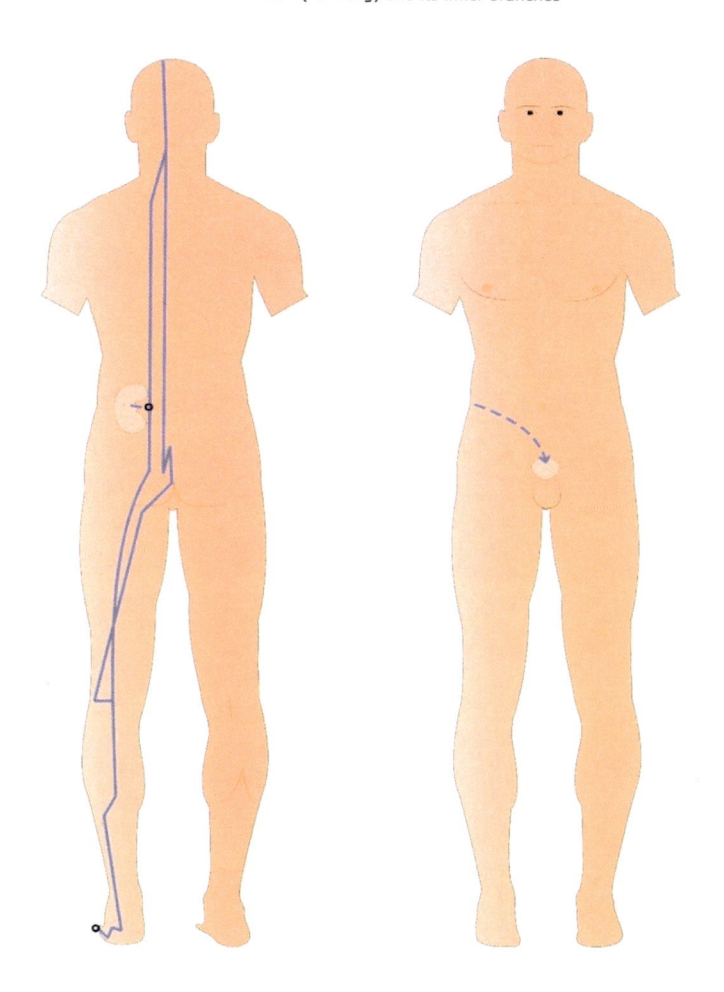

Fig. 4 – The Urinary Bladder acupuncture channel

Section 4 – Muscle channels

In addition to the main acupuncture channels of the body, there also are muscle channels that correspond to the group of muscles and fascia located along the path of the main channels.

The urinary bladder and gall bladder channels both have muscle branches that run along the back. The stomach channel has a muscle branch that travels along the abdominal area thus balancing the lower back muscles.

Urinary Bladder muscle channel

- Multifidus muscle - Part of the transverso-spinalis muscle between the vertebras along the spine.
- Longissimus muscle - Part of the erector spinae muscle along the back.
- Ilio-costalis - Part of the erector spinae muscle between the posterior ribs along the back.
- Quadratus lumborum - Lower back region between the lumbar vertebras and the hips.

Gall Bladder muscle channel

- Gluteus medius - On the outer hips.
- Gluteus minimus - On the lateral hip.
- Piriformis muscle - Along the buttock region.

Stomach muscle channel

- Rectus abdominis - Along the abdomen.

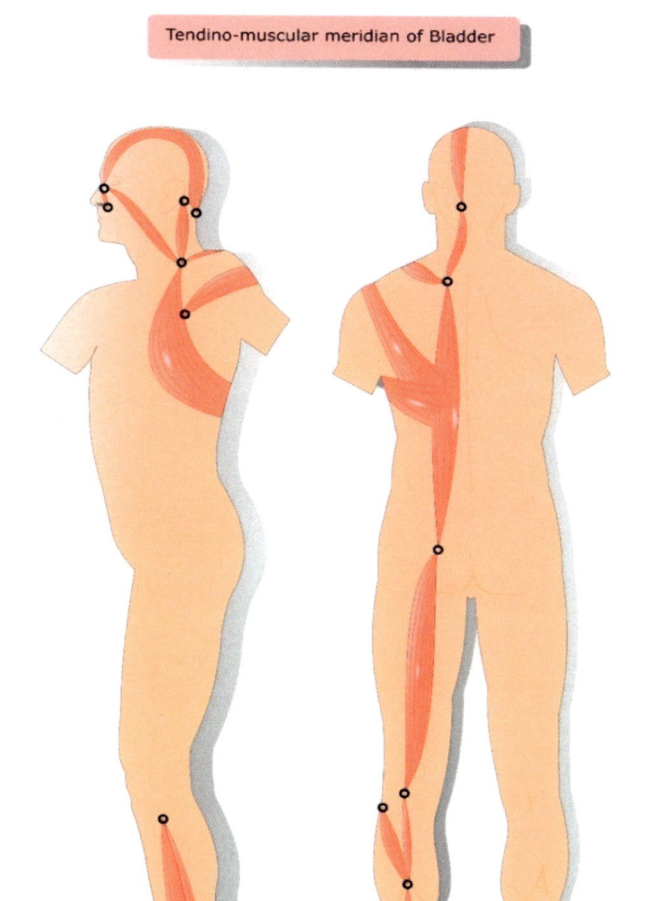

Fig. 5 – The muscle channel of the urinary bladder

In the tradition of Yoga, the lower back region also is linked to the water element and its associated psycho-energetic center the *Swadhistana Chakra* (energy vortex). This energy center, also referred to as the sacral or sex *Chakra,* is connected to the inferior hypo-gastric plexus and the sacral nerve plexus that supply nerve signals to the organs of the pelvis region. As such, the sacral energy center controls the functions of the urinary, reproductive, and hormonal systems of our body.

The *Swadhistana Chakra* is called, "One's own place or abode", because it is the abode or resting place of one's creative life force (*Kundalini*). *Kundalini* is the primal creative cosmic energy within the human body. In the physical body this primal vital force manifests as the procreative sexual energy, responsible for reproduction and the survival as a species. In the subtle body it manifests as our creative expression in the form of art, music, dance, performance, invention, inner joy, charisma, positivity, and gifted endeavors. Still, at a deeper dimension, this same force becomes the fuel and basis for unfolding one's spiritual potential.

Just as milk can be made into curd, cream, butter, or cheese, in the same manner the procreative sexual energy can manifest at various levels of expression. It is a matter of how this creative life force is channeled and utilized. In effect, one of the natural outcomes of proper spiritual cultivation is a balanced expression of the higher dimensions of this creative vital force.

The sex *Chakra* is also the seat of the unmanifest, unconscious mind, which stores our past experiences and impressions in the form of our basic instincts, drives, emotions, and desires. For this reason, lower back problems are often linked to issues concerning our instincts for safety, security, family, protection, stability, interpersonal relations, and sexuality.

Fig. 6 – Sacral Chakra

Section 5 – The mind-body connection

In the view of Qigong and Oriental medicine, there is not a clear-cut separation between the body and the mind. In effect, they are seen as a body-mind continuum and the two poles of the human being. The body is the substantial and tangible aspect of our being (Yin pole) whereas the mind is the subtle and intangible aspect (Yang pole).

Nowadays, it has been clearly established that the body and the mind directly influence one another. For instance, physiologic and biochemical imbalances in the body can affect our mental equipoise and emotional disposition. At the same time, mental stress and sustained or extreme emotions can lead to changes in the body's nervous, hormonal, and immune systems.

According to Chinese medicine, there are seven main emotional states that alter the normal flow of vital energy (chi) and directly compromise the function of the internal organs. For instance, emotions such as sadness, grief, longing, and feeling of loss weaken the function of the lungs. In turn, anxiety, worry, over-concern, and doubt bind and block the vital energy of the stomach and digestive system. Thus, the body and the mind continuously interact and influence one another.

Sustained or extreme emotions such fear, insecurity, abuse issues, self-blame, guilt, fright, dread, and shock can disturb and weaken the energy of the kidneys and adrenal glands, consequently debilitating the lower back tissues. Furthermore, memories of childhood abuse, sexual trauma, and relationship issues can be stored in the region of the lower back, resulting in blocked and constrained energy and lower back pain.

Section 6 – Main causes of lower back pain

There are a variety of disorders that can give rise to lower back pain. We can classify the causes of lower back pain into five main categories according to what tissues are involved; muscles and ligaments, lumbar vertebral joints, lumbar discs, spinal nerves, and other medical conditions.

A list of the main causes of lower back pain in both Western medicine and Oriental medicine follows below.

Western medicine

1. Muscles and ligaments

Acute lumbar muscle strain – Lumbar strain develops when the muscle fibers of the lower back are overstretched or torn due to trauma, overstretching, heavy lifting, injury, or over-strain. It results in contraction of the soft tissues, inflammation, and spasms of the back muscles.

Lumbar sprain - This condition refers to a sprain or tear of a lower back ligament. It is usually caused by injury or a sudden twisting motion of the back in which the ligament is stretched beyond its normal range of motion.

Spinal ligament syndrome - It refers to weakness of the ligaments that help support and stabilize the structure of the lower back. It commonly results from overuse, or repetitive motion of a group of muscles and ligaments that makes them weak, lax, and unbalanced. It can also develop over time from faulty posture and incorrect body mechanics that create an uneven load distribution, which places excessive weight and pressure upon the lower back region. This condition is also called overuse syndrome, repetitive strain injury, or ligament laxity.

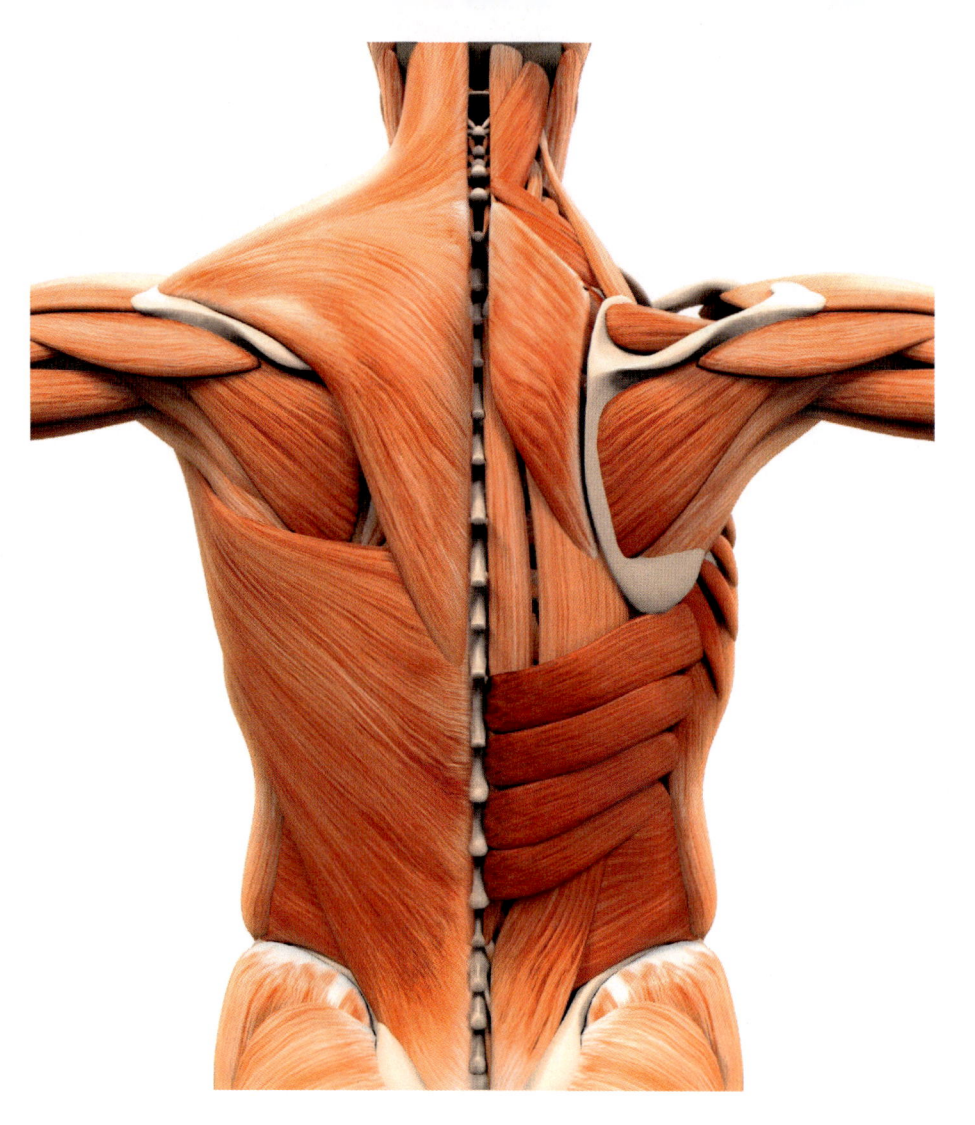

Fig. 7 – Main muscles along the back

2. Discs

Herniated or slipped lumbar disc - This condition refers to a bulging of the jelly-like collagenous material inside the center of the disc. Discs serve as shock and force absorbers between adjacent vertebras. When the disc bulges out it places pressure on the lower back ligaments and the spinal nerve roots.

Degenerative disc disease – This disorder is the result of wear, tear, thinning, and degenerative changes of the discs between the vertebras. It is a condition that develops progressively over time and leads to degenerative changes in the lumbar discs such as loss of fluid in the discs, micro tears and cracks, and bone spurs.

3. Vertebral joints

Osteoarthritis of the lower back - It refers to chronic degenerative changes of the lower back vertebras and facet joints between the vertebras. This condition involves wear and breaking down of the cartilage of the joints, resulting in calcification and the formation of bony projections known as osteophytes. It is sometimes also called degenerative joint disease or degenerative arthritis.

Spondylitis - Inflammation of the vertebral joints. It may involve one or several joints of the body.

Spondylosis - A general term used to describe any degenerative condition of the spine, which may result in calcification and the formation of bony projections known as osteophytes. It is also called osteoarthritis of the spine, or degenerative arthritis.

Spondylolithesis – Severe degenerative disorder of the facet joints causing one vertebral body to slip forward on an adjacent vertebra below it.

Stenosis of the lumbar vertebras – This disorder refers to narrowing of the vertebral spaces in the lower back, which creates pressure on the spinal nerve roots or the spinal cord. Usually, it is due to chronic inflammatory processes, calcification, and degenerative changes of the vertebras.

4. Spinal nerves

Spinal nerve root pain - It refers to compression of the spinal nerve roots commonly caused by a bulging disc, vertebral joint disease, or ligament tissue.

Sciatic pain – This refers to pressure and irritation on the sciatic nerve. The sciatic nerve originates from the two lower lumbar vertebras (L 4-5) and the first three sacral vertebras (S1-3). It is the larger and thicker nerve of the body, beginning in the lower back and sacrum and running down the buttocks area and lower extremities.

There are three main areas that can create pressure and irritation on the sciatic nerve; the lower back vertebras and sacral vertebras, the sacroiliac joint (the junction between the sacrum and the hip), and the piriformis muscle on the buttocks (piriformis syndrome). Sciatic nerve pain most commonly develops as a consequence or further complication of lower back issues.

5. Other medical conditions

Scoliosis – It refers to a lateral S curvature of the spine. Commonly, it is a congenital disorder present from birth. It also can result from an unstable sacroiliac joint or a congenital short leg condition. Other possible causes include traumatic injury to the spine and osteoporosis (thinning of the bones). In Chinese medicine this condition is associated with weak kidney energy.

Rheumatoid arthritis – It is an autoimmune disorder in which the body's immune system produces antibodies against proteins in the synovial fluid membrane of the joints, attacking its own tissues. It causes chronic inflammation and structural changes of the affected joints.

Ankylosing spondylitis – It refers to an autoimmune disorder that causes chronic inflammation that may affect the vertebras on the spine, the sacroiliac joint, and other major joints.

DISC DEGENERATION

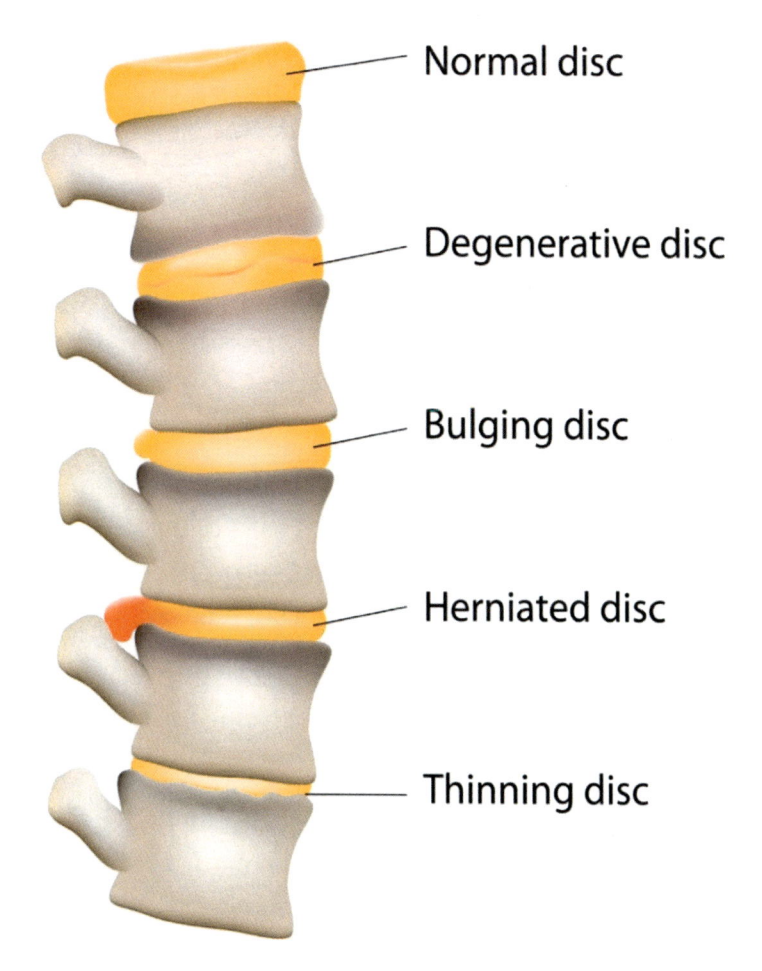

Fig. 8 – Lower back disc disorders

Oriental medicine and Qigong

In Oriental medicine back pain is differentiated according to the specific signs of the condition, the main acupuncture channels involved, and the underlying root imbalance of the symptoms.

1. Acute injury or trauma - Trauma to the lower back region characterized by stasis of blood and chi, localized inflammation, and pain.

2. Tightness and contraction of the soft tissues - Long-standing tightness and contraction of soft tissues, including the lumbar muscles and supporting ligaments. It occurs from recurrent lower back muscle strain, repetitive stress, poor posture, heavy lifting, overstretching, incorrect body mechanics, and internal organ disorders.

3. Weakness of the kidney Chi - The lower back area is considered "the residence of the kidneys". The kidneys control the circulation of vital energy and blood to the lower back tissues. Signs of weak kidney chi include poor muscle tone and weakness of the lumbar tissues, soreness and coldness of the lower back, frequent urination, and decreased stamina.

4. Muscle weakness and imbalances – This disorder involves weakness of the lower back tissues and imbalances between opposite muscle groups of the lumbar area.

5. Invasion of pathogenic cold and dampness to the lower back – This condition is caused by over-exposure to cold and damp environments. It causes stagnation of vital energy (chi) along the urinary bladder channel on the back, tightness of the lower back muscles, lumbar pain that may radiate to the hips and legs, and restricted mobility of the lower back area.

6. Stagnation of Chi in the urinary bladder channel – It is characterized by tightness and stiffness of the lower back, tenderness of the lower back muscles, limited extension and rotation of the lower back, and back pain that can radiate to the buttocks and legs.

7. Disorders of the Large intestine – The large intestine is located in the lower abdomen and the pelvic region. Disorders such as inflammation of the intestines, food sensitivities, irritable bowel syndrome, and constipation can place undue pressure upon neighboring tissues and shift the proper structure of the lower back, in turn giving rise to irritation of the lumbar spinal nerves and lower back pain.

At the same time, the large intestine acupuncture channel has connections with the abdominal, lumbar, and hamstring muscle groups that can affect the integrity of the lower back. Furthermore, the acupuncture reflex or associated point (*shu point*) of the large intestine is located between the fourth and fifth lumbar vertebras on the lower back. In this way, large intestine disorders often are reflected on the lower back.

8. Pelvic congestion - Disorders of the pelvic organs (uterus, ovaries and bladder in women, and prostate, testis and bladder in men) may elicit pressure on the lower back tissues, in particular on the sacrum region and lower spine. In addition, the acupuncture reflex or associated points (*shu point*) of the urinary bladder and reproductive organs are located on the second and fourth sacral foramens.

9. Weak abdominal muscles – The abdominal muscles help to balance and support the lower back muscles. Weaknesses and imbalances between opposite muscle groups of the lower back region are a frequent cause of chronic lower back problems. They may involve weakness of the psoas muscle and the back chain of muscles including lower back, gluteus and hamstrings muscles. Also, tightness of the muscles of the hamstrings, quadriceps, and hips can place undue pressure on the lower back.

10. Sedentary life style and lack of regular exercise - For example, continuing sitting and standing. Prolonged sitting weakens the abdominal muscles and core tissues making them unable to counterbalance the lower back muscles. Standing for long periods of time makes the gluteus minimus muscle and hip tissues tight, restricting blood circulation to the legs and lower back region.

11. Fear and anxiety – Fear-based emotions unsettle the original chi and weaken the kidney chi.

12. Relationship issues – Conflicts in interpersonal relations, in particular issues concerning intimate relations and female-male interactions, often show on the lower back area.

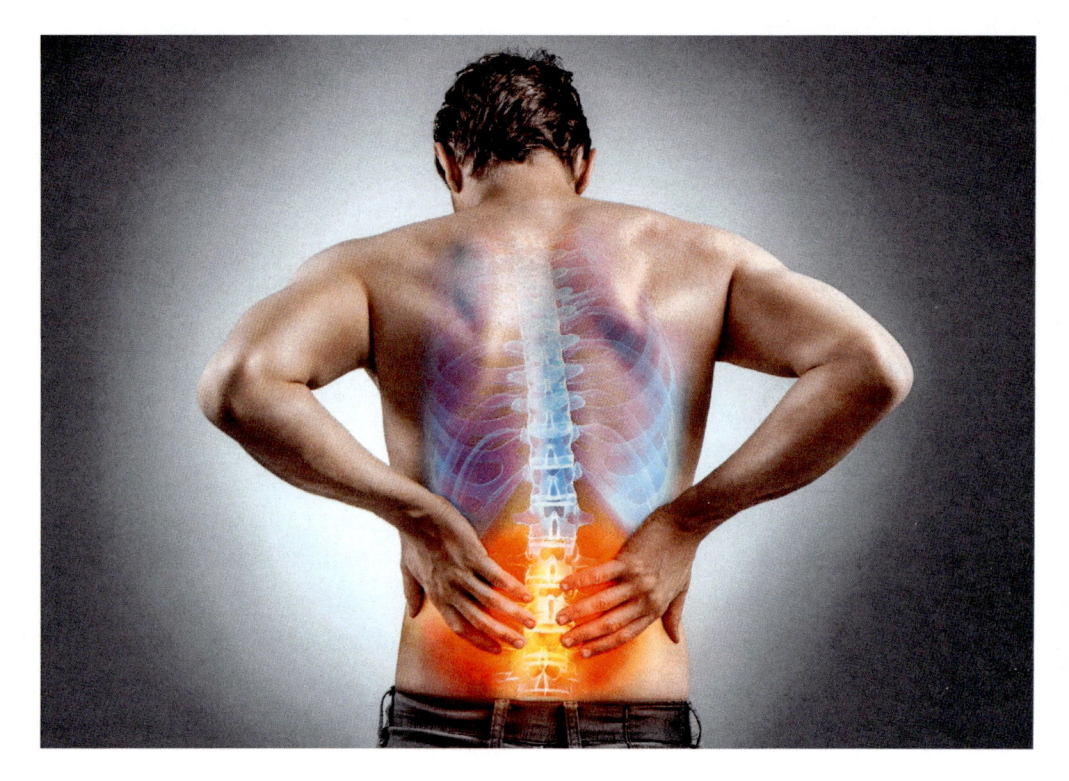

Fig. 9 – Lower back pain

Section 7 – Life style recommendations

- Use proper body mechanics when standing, sitting, or lifting.

- Be cautious not to overstrain your back by heavy lifting. When lifting weigh bend your knees and use your legs and not your back. Avoid twisting your body while lifting.

- Avoid activities that place strain on the lower back such as prolonged sitting, standing for long periods of time, repeated bending down, and sudden twisting of the body.

- Avoid standing in the same position for long periods of time. When standing make sure to maintain proper alignment of the back, shift the weight between the two legs, and turn and stretch the waist.

- When driving long distances take a break every couple of hours to move about and stretch your back.

- Stay physically active and engage in regular and moderate exercise. Incorporate exercises that strengthen the lower back.

- Control your body weight, in particular from your abdominal region so as to prevent placing undue pressure on the lower back.

- Keep your stress levels low, especially in respect to emotions such as insecurity, fear, and anxiety. Develop trust in the ultimate goodness of life and an unshakable feeling of courage and security within.

- Take care of your digestive and intestinal health through proper nutrition, avoiding foods that may promote inflammation of the intestines and maintaining good elimination.

- If suspecting, check for food sensitivities (Ig-G, IgG4, and LRA blood tests).

- Promote pelvic circulation. In particular, women should keep the pelvic area free of congestion by incorporating exercises like deep breathing, Tai Chi, Qigong, and Yoga.

- Avoid overuse of stimulants like coffee, sugar, energy drinks, and recreational drugs that place a burden upon the adrenal glands and the kidneys.

- Be cautious of overindulgence in sex, in particular frequent ejaculation for men.

- Get enough sleep and go to sleep at regular times. Ideally, go to sleep not later than 10:00 pm. Not getting enough sleep and going late to sleep affects the adrenals, kidneys, and liver functions.

Section 8 – Notes on practicing the exercises

1. The exercises presented in this instructional guide can be used both as a preventative and therapeutic exercise program. However, some of the exercises may be contraindicated in certain disorders or conditions. Please, follow the specific instructions, observations, precautions, and contraindications for each exercise.

2. The exercises can be practiced in three ways.

    - As individual exercises based on their specific indications and benefits.

    - As a group of three to six complementary exercises to address a particular health complaint.

    - As a complete exercise set to help prevent and maintain neck, shoulders, and upper back health.

3. In most situations it is not necessary practicing all the exercises in the set. Select the exercises that are indicated for your specific condition and that target the affected areas. In the majority of cases a combination of three to six exercises will address most common complaints.

4. Always use caution and listen to your body when introducing a new exercise program. If any pain or discomfort arises discontinue the exercise.

5. The exercises should be adapted to your particular state of health and physical condition.

6. First, practice the exercises slowly and gently. Then, once you have familiarity with them, you can perform the exercises more fluently.

7. Practice the selected exercises once or twice a day, repeating each exercise several times as indicated in the exercise description.

8. Follow the specific instructions, observations, precautions, and contraindications for each exercise.

9. Select a balanced and well-rounded combination of exercises. Avoid practicing more than three exercises in a row that work the same muscle groups. Alternate exercises that work opposite muscles groups e.g. extensor and flexors. Also, incorporate exercises that both lengthen and strengthen the affected areas.

10. In severe cases of lower back pain it is recommended that you consult with your doctor or primary health care provider, in order to determine the safety and suitability of the exercises.

Section 9 – Description of the exercises

1. SOOTHING THE WAIST

Description of the exercise

1. Stand with the feet shoulder-width apart, hips tucked, back straight, and knees bent.

2. Place the palms on the navel with arms relaxed (Fig. 1.1).

3. Slowly, turn the waist to the left side (Fig. 1.2).

4. Turn the waist back to the initial position (Fig. 1.1).

5. Slowly, turn the waist to the right side (Fig. 1.3).

6. Turn the waist back to the initial position (Fig. 1.1).

7. Repeat turning the waist to the left and right sides several times.

Figs. 1.1 and 1.2

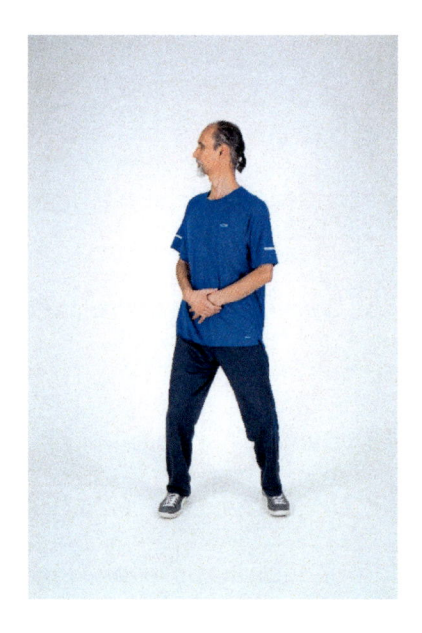

Fig. 1.3

Common mistakes

- ➢ Thrusting the pelvis forward.
- ➢ Turning the waist forcefully.
- ➢ Turning from the shoulders.
- ➢ Turning the hips excessively.

Precautions and contraindications

1. Adjust the degree of turning the waist according to the state of health of your back.

Main benefits

- Helps loosening the lower back region.

- Improves the range of motion of the lower back area.
- Relieves stiffness of the lower back.
- Exercises the abdominal region

2. LUBRICATING THE WAIST

Description of the exercise

1. Stand with the feet shoulder-width apart.

2. Turn the right foot out 45-60 degrees, shift weight to the right leg, and take one step forward with the left foot into a left front-bow stance. Keep the weight on the right leg and the feet shoulder-width apart.

3. Place the hands in front of the abdomen with the palms facing the body. Hold the knees bent (Fig. 2.1).

4. Slowly, turn the waist to the left side, shifting weight into the left leg (Fig. 2.2).

5. Slowly, turn the waist to the right side, shifting weight back into the right leg (Fig. 2.1).

6. Alternate turning the waist to the left and right sides several times.

7. Step back with the left foot into a parallel stance. Turn the left foot out 45-60 degrees, shift weight into the left leg, and take one step forward with the right foot into a right front- bow stance. Keep the weight on the left leg and feet shoulder-width apart.

8. Place the hands in front of the abdomen with the palms facing the body. Hold the knees bent (Fig. 2.3).

9. Repeat the exercise on the right side (Figs. 2.3 and 2.4).

Figs. 2.1 and 2.2

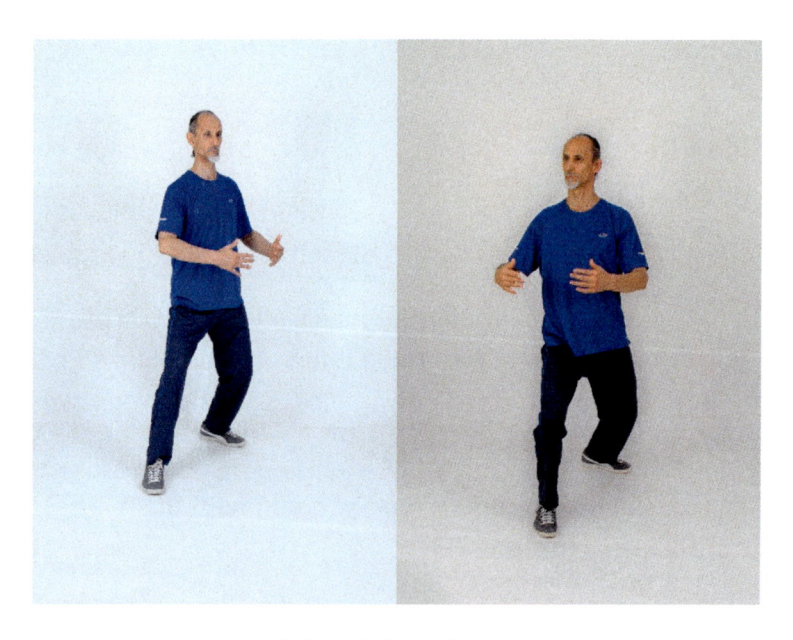

Figs. 2.3 and 2.4

Common mistakes

- ➤ Turning from the hips instead of the waist.
- ➤ Excessive movement of the shoulders.
- ➤ Moving the arms independently from turning the body.
- ➤ Arching the back.
- ➤ Turning the hip or knee inward on the empty leg.
- ➤ Tightening the lower back.

Main benefits

- Loosens the waist and lower back area.
- Relieves stiffness and tightness of the lower back.
- Stimulates energy flow and blood circulation to the lower back region.
- Warms the lower back area.
- Increases the range of motion of the waist and lower back.
- Strengthens the kidneys and adrenals glands.

3. OVERHEAD ARM STRETCH

Description of the exercise

1. Stand with the feet shoulder-width apart and head upright.

2. Bend the left arm behind the body with the dorsum of the hand resting on the back (Fig. 3.1)

Fig. 3.1

3. Raise the right arm up the side to shoulder level with palm facing up. Continuing the movement bring the arm straight up over the head, following the movement of the hand with the eyes. Hold the right palm up with the fingers facing back (Figs. 3.2 and 3.3).

Figs. 3.2 and 3.3

4. Push the right palm up at the same time lifting the chest and pulling the tailbone down. Look up at the hand (Fig. 3.3).

5. Hold the position for 10 seconds.

6. Lower the right arm down the side to shoulder level, following the movement with the eyes. (Fig. 3.4).

7. Continuing the movement bring the right hand down the side and then behind the back, eyes looking straight to the front (Fig. 3.5).

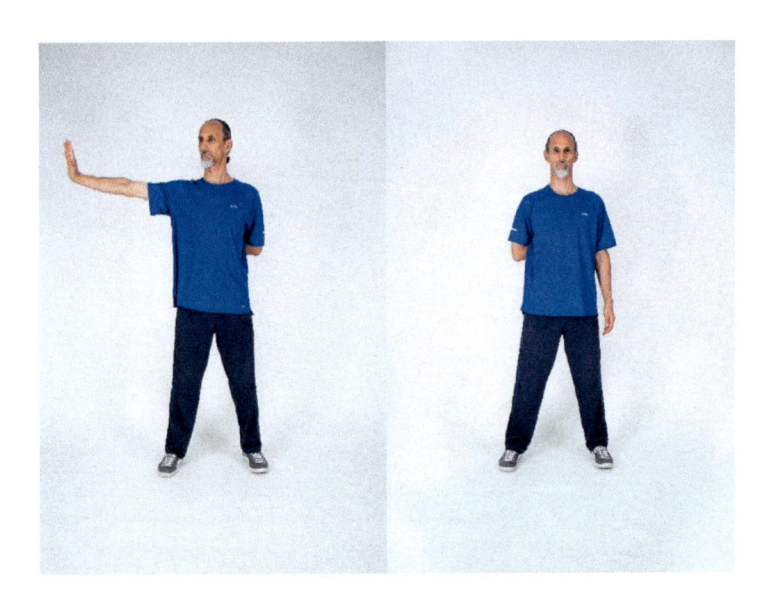

Figs. 3.4 and 3.5

8. Repeat the exercise with the left hand (Figs. 3.6, 3.7, and 3.8).

9. Inhale when raising the hand, hold the breath or breathe naturally when pushing up the hand, and exhale when lowering the hand.

10. Alternate the exercise with the right and left hands three times.

Figs. 3.6 and 3.7

Fig. 3.8

11. Next, turning the right palm up, raise the right arm up the side and straight over the head. The hand ends with the palm down facing the forehead and the right elbow slightly bent (Fig. 3.9).

12. Continuing the movement turn the body about 45-60 degrees to the left side and look up at the right palm (Fig. 3.10).

13. Hold the position for three breaths, focusing on the right palm when exhaling and on the lower back region (life gate area) when inhaling (Fig. 3.10).

14. Bring the right palm down facing the front of the body and then turn the body back to the front (Fig. 3.11).

Fig. 3.9

Figs. 3.10 and 3.11

15. Bring the right arm behind the body with the dorsum of the hand resting on the back (Fig. 3.5).

16. Turning the left palm up, raise the left arm up the side and straight over the head. The left hand should end with the palm down facing the forehead and the left elbow slightly bent (Fig. 3.12).

17. Continuing the movement, turn the body about 45-60 degrees to the right side and look up at the left palm (Fig. 3.13).

18. Hold the position for three breaths, focusing on the left palm when exhaling and on the lower back region (life gate area) when inhaling (Fig. 3.13).

19. Bring the left palm down facing the front of the body and then turn the body back to the initial position (Fig. 3.14).

Fig. 3.12

Figs. 3.13 and 3.14

Observations

1. When holding the hand above the head push with the palm at the same time tensing the arm, thrusting the chest, and pulling the tailbone down.

Common mistakes

- ➢ Thrusting the pelvis forward.
- ➢ Raising the shoulders.
- ➢ Failure lifting the chest and pulling down the sacrum.
- ➢ Contracting the neck.
- ➢ Raising the hips.

Precautions and contraindications

1. This exercise may be contraindicated for people with rotator-cuff injuries or painful conditions of the shoulders.

Main benefits

- It gently pulls the two ends of the spine thus lengthening the back.
- Stretches the whole back.
- Relieves tightness and stiffness of the lower back.
- Helps stabilize and strengthen the lower back.
- It tones the lower back area.
- Stretches the upper back, shoulder blade, shoulder, and neck areas.
- Promotes energy flow and blood circulation to the lower back and the kidneys.
- Activates the flow of vital energy along the central channel in the spine.

4. LOTUS LEAF SWAYING ON THE WIND

Description of the exercise

1. Stand with the feet slightly wider than the shoulders.

2. Place the hands on the hips with the thumbs pressing on the lower back area and the four fingers pointing to the front (Fig. 4.1).

3. Rotate the waist to the front, left side, back, right side, and front, making a complete circle (Figs. 4.2, 4.3, 4.4, 4.5, 4.6, 4.7, 4.8, and 4.9)

4. Repeat the movement several times.

5. Change the direction of the movement rotating the waist to the right side, back, left side, and front, making a complete circle (Figs. 4.5, 4.4, 4.3, 4.2, 4.9, 4.8, 4.7, and 4.6).

6. Repeat the movement several times.

7. When rotating toward the back inhale and when rotating toward the front exhale.

Fig. 4.1

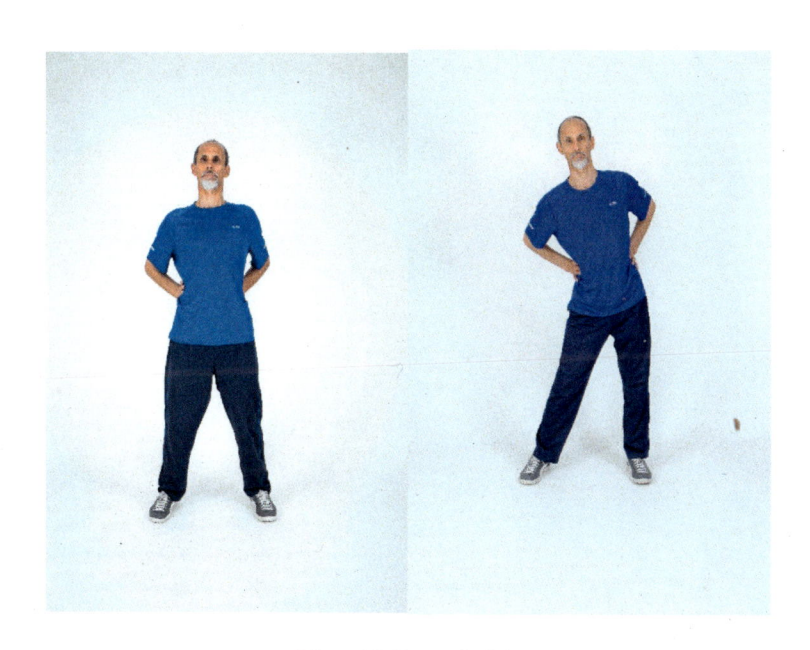

Figs. 4.2 and 4.3

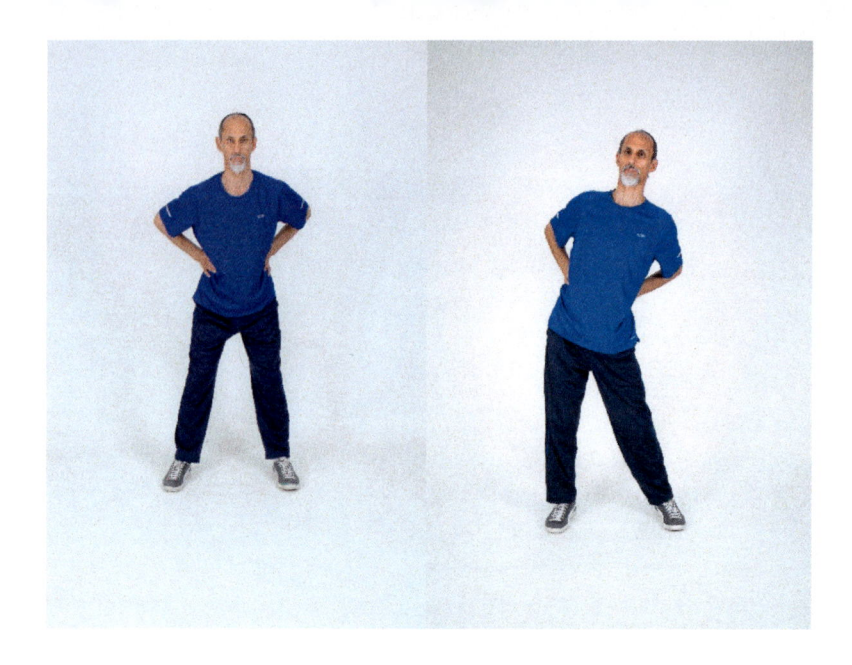

Figs. 4.4 and 4.5

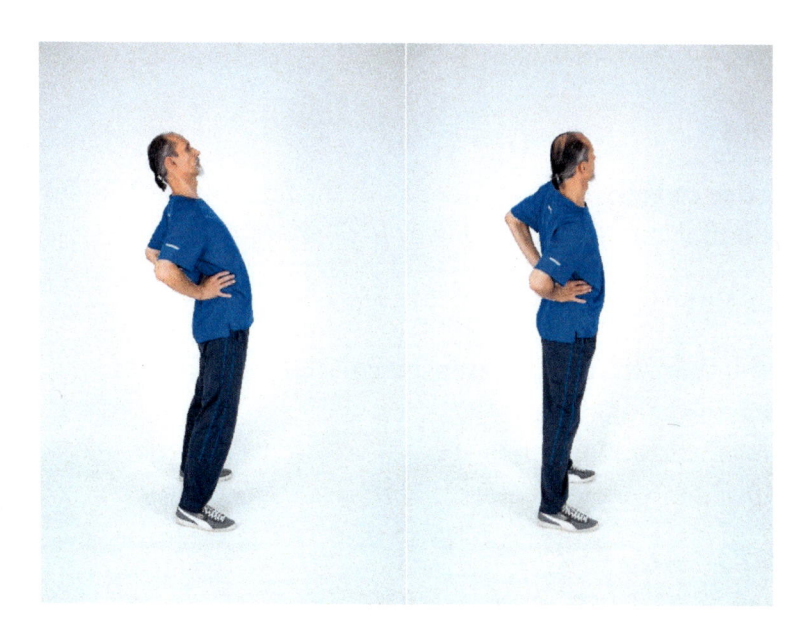

Figs. 4.6 and 4.7

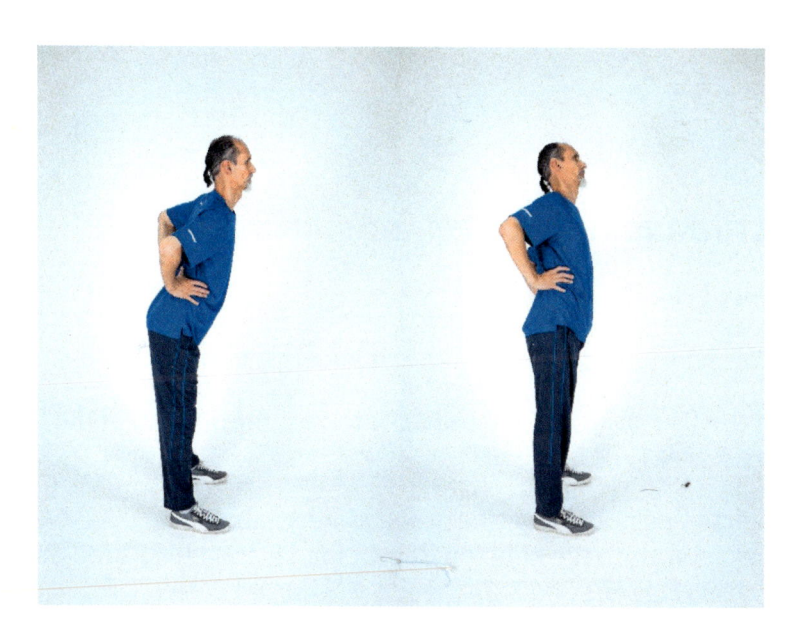

Figs. 4.8 and 4.9

Observations

1. This exercise can also be performed with the feet together, knees straight, and the palms flat supporting the lower back area.

Common mistakes

- ➢ Rotating from the shoulders instead of the waist.
- ➢ Moving the trunk excessively.
- ➢ Moving the head forward.
- ➢ Making an incomplete rotation of the waist.

Main benefits

- Loosens up and improves flexibility of the back.
- Releases stiffness, tightness, and achiness of the lower back area.
- Improves mobility of the lower back region.
- Increases the range of motion of the lower spine.
- Promotes energy flow and blood circulation to the lower back tissues.
- Stimulates kidney function.

5. STRENGTHENING THE KIDNEYS AND GUIDING CHI

Description of the exercise

1. Stand with feet slightly wider that the shoulders and the knees bent.

2. Making loose fists bring the hands back and rest the dorsum of the hands on the lower back area (Fig. 5.1).

3. While holding this position perform six breaths, inhaling to the lower back region and exhaling into the kidneys. Repeat for six breaths or until the kidney area feels warm (Figs. 5.1 and 5.4).

4. Next, turn the waist to the left side and look behind the left shoulder to the rear as you inhale (Figs. 5.2 and 5.5).

5. Return to the starting position as you exhale (Figs. 5.1 and 5.4).

6. Turn the waist to the right side and look behind the right shoulder to the rear as you inhale (Figs. 5.3 and 5.6).

7. Return to the starting position as you exhale.

8. Repeat turning the waist to the left and right sides for six times (Figs. 5.1, 5.2, and 5.3).

9. End the exercise bringing the hands to the lower abdomen.

Figs 5.1

Figs. 5.2 and 5.3

Fig. 5.4

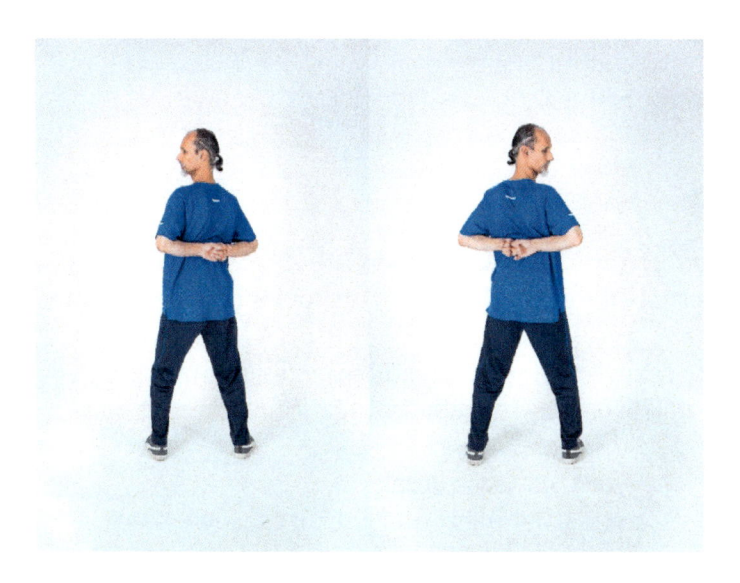

Figs 5.5 and 5.6

Observations

1. Hold the lower back area relaxed and rounded, preventing arching of the back.

2. Keep the shoulders relaxed and lowered.

3. Make sure to turn from the waist instead of the shoulders.

Precautions and contraindications

1. Do not practice this exercise if having a cold, fever, congestion, or acute infectious disease.

Common mistakes

- ➢ Arching the back.
- ➢ Thrusting the pelvis forward.
- ➢ Raising the shoulders.
- ➢ Thrusting the chest forward

➤ Turning from the shoulders instead of the waist.
➤ Twisting or contracting the neck.
➤ Tightening the hips.

Main benefits

- Strengthens the kidneys.
- Guides vital energy (chi) down to the lower back, stimulating kidney functions.
- Helps to relieve signs of nephritis, impotence, premature ejaculation, menstrual disorders, menopausal symptoms, depression, tinnitus, and cold limbs.
- Relaxes the waist and back areas.
- Relieves soreness, tightness, and pain of the lower back.
- Helps warming the kidneys and the life gate area on the lower back (*ming men*).
- Stimulates overall energy and vitality.
- Promotes hormonal production.
- Helps balancing the hormones and the reproductive system.

6. BENDING AND TURNING THE TRUNK

Description of the exercise

1. Stand with feet slightly wider than the shoulders.

2. Place the right hand on the lower abdomen and the left hand on the lower back, both palms facing up (Fig. 6.1).

3. Turn left, then bend the body about ninety degrees down the left side, extending the right hand out in front (Figs. 6.2 and 6.3).

4. Continuing the movement, turn the body to the right extending both hands out the sides, then moving the left hand forward and the right hand back (Figs 6.4, 6.5, and 6.6).

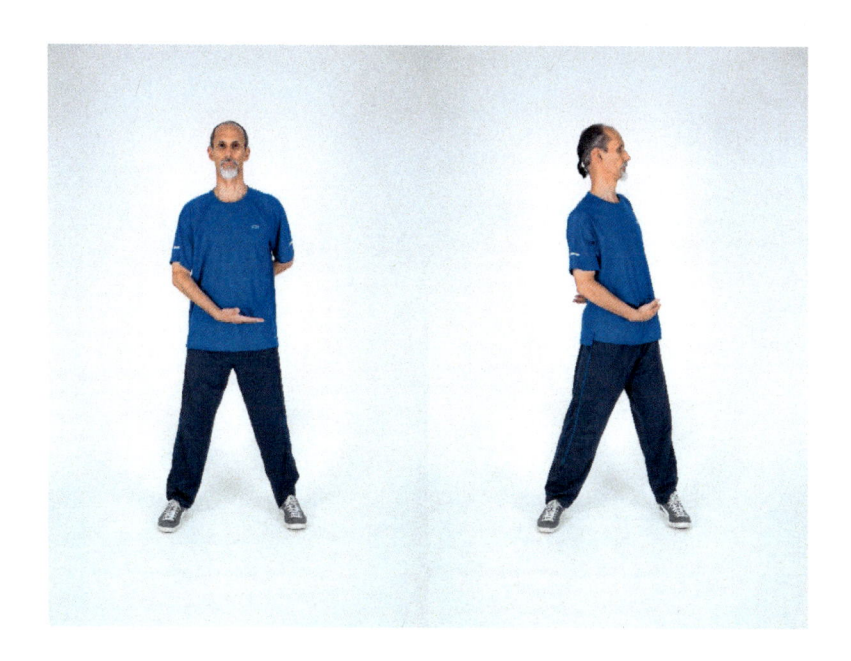

Figs. 6.1 and 6.2

Figs. 6.3 and 6.4

Figs. 6.5 and 6.6

5. Straightening the body up the right side, bring the left hand up above the head with palm down and the right hand to the lower back with palm up. Then, bend the body sideways to the right (Figs 6.7 and 6.8).

6. Turn the body back to the initial position and bring the left hand down to the lower abdomen with palm facing up (Fig. 6.9).

Figs. 6.7 and 6.8

Fig. 6.9

7. Turn right, then bend the body about ninety degrees down the right side, extending the left hand out in front (Figs. 6.10 and 6.11).

8. Continuing the movement, turn the body to the left extending both hands out the sides, then moving the right hand forward and the left hand back (Figs. 6.12, 6.13, and 6.14).

Figs. 6.10 and 6.11

Figs. 6.12 and 6.13

Fig. 6.14

9. Straightening the body up the left side, bring the right hand up above the head with palm down and the left hand to the lower back with palm up. Then, bend the body sideways to the left (Figs. 6.15 and 6.16).

10. Turn the body back to the initial position and bring the right hand down to the lower abdomen with palm facing up (Fig. 6.17).

11. Repeat the movement to the left and right sides several times.

Figs. 6.15 and 6.16

Fig. 6.17

Precautions and contraindications

1. This exercise may be contraindicated for people with acute or severe lower back pain, herniated disc, sciatic nerve pain, high blood pressure, vertigo, and abdominal hernias.

2. Adjust the degree of bending and turning the body according to your state of health and physical condition.

Common mistakes

- ➢ Hunching the lower back when bending the body.
- ➢ Turning from the shoulders instead of the waist.
- ➢ Tightening or raising the shoulders.
- ➢ Twisting the hips when turning the body.

➤ Not extending or straightening the back.

Main benefits

- Stretches the lower back area.
- Helps lengthening the spine.
- Increases flexibility of the lower back.
- Improves the range of motion of the lower back.
- Stretches the upper back and shoulder blades area.

7. BEAR TURNING AND LOOKING BACK

Description of the exercise

1. Stand with the feet shoulder-width apart, back straight, hips tucked, and knees bent.

2. Bring the hands to the sides of the body at hips level with the palms facing down and fingers pointing to the front. Keep the elbows off-lock (Fig. 7.1).

3. Turn the waist to the left side, gently pushing down with the right palm. At the same time turn the head and gaze to the rear and down (Fig. 7.2).

4. Turn the waist to the right side, gently pushing down with the left palm. At the same time turn the head and gaze to the rear and down (Fig.7.3).

5. When turning to the sides inhale and when moving back to the initial position exhale.

6. Repeat the movement several times (Figs. 7.1, 7.2, and 7.3).

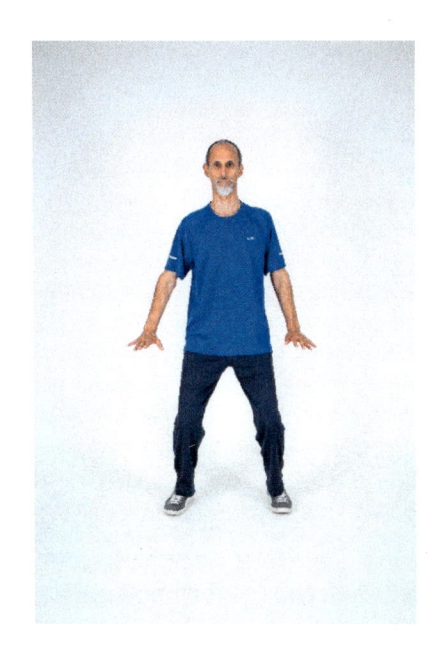

Fig. 7.1

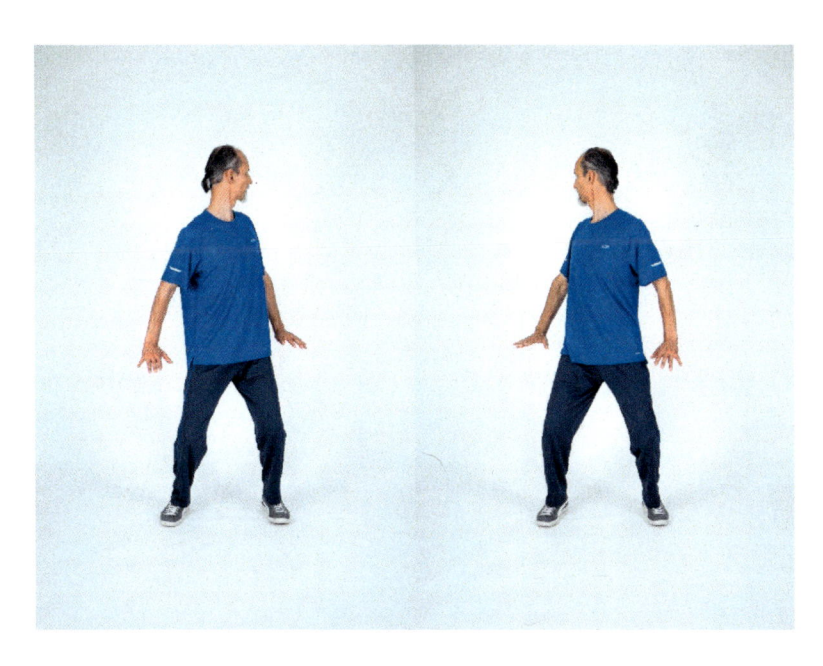

Figs. 7.2 and 7.3

Common mistakes

- ➤ Sticking out the buttocks.
- ➤ Arching the back.
- ➤ Turning from the shoulders instead of the waist.
- ➤ Turning the hips excessively.
- ➤ Twisting the hips.
- ➤ Straightening the knees.
- ➤ Raising the shoulders.

Main benefits

- Lengthens and stretches the lower back area.
- Increases mobility of the lower back.
- Helps stabilizing and strengthening the lower back.
- Promotes energy flow and blood circulation to the lower back region.
- Stimulates and strengthens kidney function.
- Releases tension and tightness of the lower back region.

8. BENDING THE TRUNK AND STRETCHING THE ARMS

Description of the exercise

1. Stand with the feet slightly wider than the shoulders.

2. Interlock the hands in front of the lower abdomen with palms facing up (Fig. 8.1).

Fig. 8.1

3. Bring the hands up to chest level then rotate them out and straight up, extending the hands over the head (Figs. 8.2 and 8.3).

Figs. 8.2 and 8.3

4. Bring the hands down to chest level with palms up (Fig. 8.4).

Fig. 8.4

5. Turn to the left and bend the body down the left side. Then, rotate the hands out and extend the hands down the side (Figs. 8.5 and 8.6).

6. Bend the knees and straighten the body up the left side at the same time turning the palms out and curving the back (Fig. 8.7).

Figs. 8.5 and 8.6

Fig. 8.7

7. Turn the body back to the starting position, bringing the hands to chest level with palms up (Fig. 8.8).

8. Turn to the right and bend the body down the right side. Then, rotate the hands out and extend the hands down the side (Figs. 8.9 and 8.10).

Fig. 8.8

Figs. 8.9 and 8.10

9. Bend the knees and straighten the body up the right side at the same time curving the back (Fig. 8.11).

10. Turn the body back to the starting position, bringing the hands to chest level with palms up (Fig. 8.12)

Figs. 8.11 and 8.12

11. Bend the body down the front, rotating and extending the hands down (Fig. 8.13).

12. Bend the knees and straighten up the body at the same time curving the back (Fig. 8.14).

13. Repeat the complete sequence two times more.

Figs. 8.13 and 8.14

Common mistakes

- ➢ Bending from the waist instead of the hips.
- ➢ Failure stabilizing and pushing back the hips.
- ➢ Not lengthening the lower back when bending down.
- ➢ Dropping the arms too early when bending the body.
- ➢ Not bending the knees or bowing the back when straightening the body.

Precautions and contraindications

1. This exercise should not be performed in cases of acute lower back pain, herniated or slipped lumbar disc, and sciatic pain.
2. This exercise should be practiced with caution in cases of high blood pressure, vertigo, dizziness, stroke, glaucoma, heart disease, and hernias.

Main benefits

- Increases flexibility of the lower back.

- Stretches the lower back area and the hamstring muscles.
- Helps strengthening the back.
- Relieves stiffness, achiness, and pain of the lower back and legs.
- Helps lengthening the back.

9. PUSHING ON BACK

Description of the exercise

1. Stand with the feet shoulder-width apart and hands by the sides.

2. Turn the body 90 degrees to the left, pivoting on the left heel (Fig. 9.1).

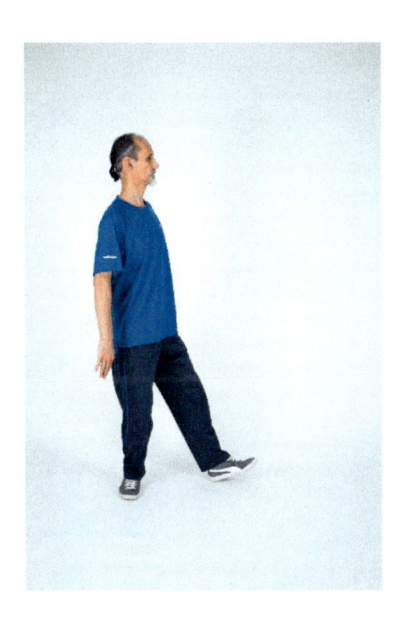

Fig. 9.1

3. Shift weight to the left leg, lifting the right heel as you raise the arms up to chest level (Fig. 9.2).

4. Shift weight back to the right leg, lifting the left toes and bringing the palms to the lower back as you tuck the hips (Fig. 9.3).

Figs. 9.2 and 9.3

5. Again, shift weight to the left leg lifting the right heel as you arch the lower back (Fig. 9.4).

6. Shift weight back to the right leg, tucking the hips and lifting the left toes (Fig. 9.3).

Figs. 9.4 and 9.3

7. Return to the starting position.

8. Turn the body 90 degrees to the right, pivoting on the right heel (Fig. 9.5).

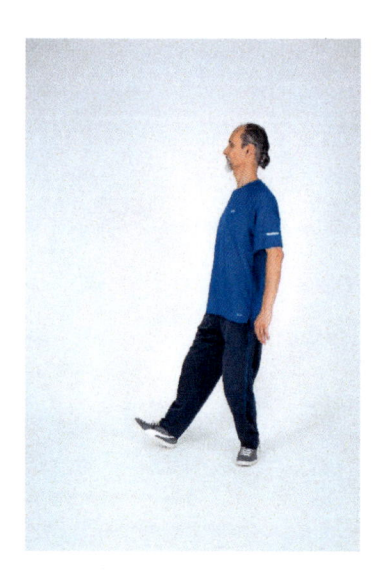

Fig. 9.5

9. Shift the weight to the right leg, lifting the left heel as you raise the arms up to chest level (Fig. 9.6).

10. Shift weight back to the left leg, lifting the right toes and bringing the palms to the lower back as you tuck the hips (Fig. 9.7).

Figs. 9.6 and 9.7

11. Again, shift the weight to the right leg, lifting the left heel as you arch the lower back (Fig. 9.8).

12. Shift weight back to the left leg, tucking the hips and lifting the right toes (Fig. 9.7).

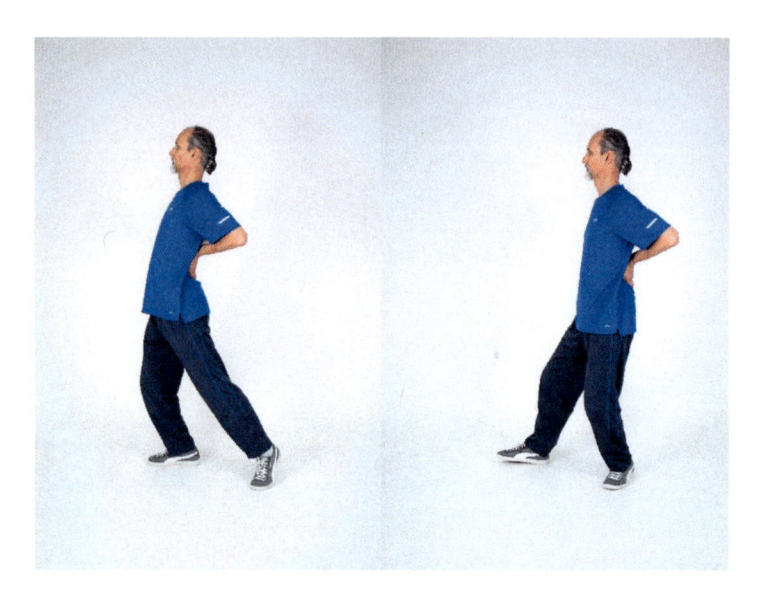

Figs. 9.8 and 9.7

13. Return to the starting position.

14. Repeat the exercise to the left and right sides two times more.

Common mistakes

- ➢ Raising the shoulders.
- ➢ Not tucking and arching the back.
- ➢ Lack of coordination between the movements of the hands, legs, and back.

Main benefits

- Increases flexibility of the lower back region.
- Helps extending and flexing the lower spine.
- Relieves soreness and stiffness of the lower back.
- Stretches the pelvis, abdomen, and chest.

10. STANDING LOCUST

Description of the exercise

1. Stand with the feet shoulder-width apart and hands by the sides (Fig. 10.1).

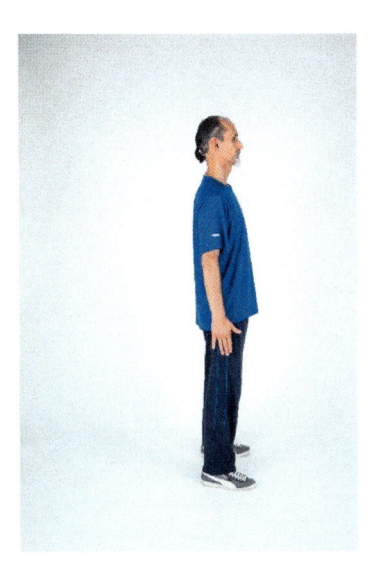

Fig. 10.1

2. Shift weight into the left leg. Then, extend the right leg straight back. At the same time extend the arms back behind the body with the palms facing each other (Fig. 10.2).

3. Hold the position for 10-15 seconds.

4. Bring the right leg back to the initial position.

5. Shift weight into the right leg. Then, extend the left leg straight back. At the same time extend the arms back behind the body with the palms facing each other (Fig. 10.3).

6. Hold the position for 10-15 seconds.

7. Bring the left leg back to the initial position.

8. Alternate the exercise with the right and left legs several times (Figs. 10.1, 10.2, and 10.3).

Figs. 10.2 and 10.3

9. When extending the leg and arms inhale, when holding the position breathe naturally, and when lowering the leg and arms exhale.

Observations

1. This exercise also can be performed lifting and extending the leg back, at the same time extending the arms up above the head with palms facing each other (Figs. 10.4 and 10.5).

Figs. 10.4 and 10.5

Common mistakes

- ➢ Failure stabilizing the pelvis.
- ➢ Raising, turning, or twisting the hips.
- ➢ Leaning forward excessively when raising the leg.
- ➢ Raising the shoulders.
- ➢ Insufficient extension of the leg.

Main benefits

- Strengthens and tones the muscles and ligaments of the back.
- Strengthens the 'back chain of muscles' that supports the lower back region, including the muscles of the lower back, buttocks, and hamstrings.
- Helps correcting poor lower back curvature (lumbar lordosis).

- Helps balancing opposite muscles groups on the upper and lower back.

11. BACK STEPPING

Description of the exercise

1. Stand with the feet shoulder-width apart, head upright, and back straight.

2. Place the hands on the hips with the thumbs pressing on the lower back area and the other four fingers pointing to the front (Fig. 11.1).

Fig. 11.1

3. Raise the right knee and take a step back with the right leg, setting the toes on the ground. Then, place the rest of the foot down transferring the weigh to the right leg (Figs. 11.2, 11.3, and 11.4).

Figs. 11.2 and 11.3

Fig. 11.4

4. Step forward with the right foot back to the initial position (Fig. 11.1).

Fig. 11.1

5. Raise the left knee and take a step back with the left leg, setting the toes on the ground. Then, place the whole foot down transferring the weight to the left leg (Figs. 11.5, 11.6, and 11.7).

Figs. 11.5 and 11.6

Fig. 11.7

6. Step forward with the left foot back to the initial position (Fig. 11.1).

7. Alternate stepping back with the right and left legs at a rate of about 40 steps per minute.

8. Complete between 50 and 100 steps.

Observations

1. One also can step back while at the same time swinging the opposite arm up.

Common mistakes

- ➢ Not stabilizing the pelvis properly.
- ➢ Rising, turning, or twisting the hips when stepping back.
- ➢ Arching the back.
- ➢ Hollowing the chest.
- ➢ Lowering the head.

Main benefits

- Strengthens the lower back, buttocks, and hamstrings muscles.
- Improves tone of the lower back tissues.
- Improves the strength and stability of the spine.
- Increases the dorsal extension of the back musculature.
- Relieves lower back pain, lumbar muscle strain, and soreness of the lower back.
- Helps balancing the muscle groups on the front of the legs, such as the quadricep muscles commonly involved in walking.
- Helps correcting and preventing a hunchback posture.

Precautions and contraindications

1. The ground should be even and free of obstacles.

2. This exercise is contraindicated in cases of lower back pain caused by malignant tumors and tuberculosis.

3. Adjust the speed and duration of the exercise according to your physical condition, state of health, and age.

12. THE WARRIOR

Description of the exercise

1. Stand with the feet shoulder-width apart and hands by the sides (Fig. 12.1).

2. Bend the knees and slide the hands down the thighs, placing the weight of the body on the heels. At the same time hinge at the hips, sticking out the buttocks and arching the back (Fig. 12.2).

3. Hold this position for a few seconds then extend the arms back with palms facing each other (Fig 12.3).

4. Push the hips back and the shoulders down toward the hips. Keep the head up looking straight forward. Hold this position for about 15 seconds (Fig. 12.3).

5. Then, extend the arms up in front as high as you can. Keep the weight on the heels and the hips back. Hold this position for about 20 seconds (Fig. 12.4).

6. Slowly, straighten the body and lower the arms.

7. Repeat the exercise two times more.

Figs. 12.1 and 12.2

Figs. 12.3 and 12.4

Common mistakes

- ➢ Tucking the pelvis.
- ➢ Not flexing or hinging at the hips.
- ➢ Insufficient arching of the back.
- ➢ Placing the weight of the body on the front of the feet.
- ➢ Overextending the knees.
- ➢ Looking down.
- ➢ Raising the shoulders.

Main benefits

- Provides extension to the spine.
- Helps toning and strengthening the tissues of the lower back.
- Improves the normal curvature of the lower back (lumbar lordosis).
- Strengthens the deep postural muscle groups along the spine.
- Helps to activate the back chain of muscles that support the back, including the muscles of the buttocks, hamstrings, lower back, and upper back.

13. JADE LADY WORKS THE SHUTTLES

Description of the exercise

1. Stand with the feet wider than the shoulders and knees bent.

2. Shift weight to the left leg and bring the right hand above the left hand with palms facing as if holding a ball (Fig. 13.1).

3. Turn the waist to the right side, shifting weight to the right leg with hands as if holding a ball (Fig. 13.2).

4. Bring the left hand up to chest level placing the three middle fingers of the right hand on the inner aspect of the left wrist. Then, turn to the left side

shifting weight to the left leg and extending the arms out, spiraling up to the left side (Fig. 13.3).

5. Turn the waist to the right side, shifting weight to the right leg. At the same time bring the arms inward with hands apart, spiraling down to the right side (Fig. 13.4).

6. Turn the waist to the left side, shifting weight to the left leg. At the same time move the hands out to the left side, turning the left hand horizontally at head level and the right hand vertically at chest level, both palms facing out (Fig. 13.5).

Figs. 13.1 and 13.2

Figs. 13.3 and 13.4

Fig. 13.5

7. Turn the waist to the right side, shifting weight to the right leg. At the same time bring the left hand above the right hand with palms facing as if holding a ball (Fig. 13.6).

8. Turn the waist to the left side, shifting weight to the left leg with hands as if holding the ball (Fig. 13.7).

9. Bring the right hand up to chest level placing the three middle fingers of the left hand on the inner aspect of the right wrist. Then, turn to the right side, shifting weight to the right leg and extending the arms out, spiraling up to the right side (Fig. 13.8).

10. Turn the waist to the left side, shifting weight to the left leg. At the same time bring the arms inward with hands apart, spiraling down to the left side (Fig. 13.9).

11. Turn the waist to the right side, shifting weight to the right side. At the same time move the hands out to the right side, turning the right hand horizontally at head level and the left hand vertically at chest level, both palms facing out (Fig. 13.10).

12. Turn the waist to the left side, shifting weight to the left leg. At the same time bring the right hand above the left hand with palms facing as if holding a ball (Fig. 13.1).

13. Repeat the exercise to the left and right sides several times.

Figs. 13.6 and 13.7

Figs. 13.8 and 13.9

Fig. 13.10

Common mistakes

- ➢ Turning from the hips instead of the waist.
- ➢ Turning the shoulders excessively.
- ➢ Raising the shoulders.
- ➢ Raising the elbows.

Main benefits

- Loosens the waist area.
- Helps relieve tightness and stiffness of the lower back.
- Increases circulation to the lower back region.
- Improves mobility of the lower back.
- Stimulates the kidneys.
- Compresses and stretches the abdomen, providing a massaging action to the internal organs.

- Improves digestion.
- Helps to relieve abdominal distention, nausea, and low energy.
- It works out the lower and upper back regions.
- Increases energy level and overall vitality.

14. HEEL ON BUTTOCKS

Description of the exercise

1. Stand with feet shoulder-width apart.

2. Place the hands on the hips with the thumbs pressing on the lower back area and the four fingers facing to the front (Fig. 14.1).

3. Flex the right knee back, bringing the right heel toward the buttocks (Fig. 14.2).

4. Hold this position for about 15 seconds (Fig. 14.2).

5. Then, extend the right leg back holding it for a few seconds (Fig. 14.3).

6. Lower the right foot.

7. Flex the left knee back, bringing the left heel toward the buttocks (Fig. 14.4).

8. Hold this position for 15 seconds (Fig. 14.4).

9. Then, extend the left leg back holding it for a few seconds (Fig. 14.5).

10. Lower the left foot.

11. Repeat the exercise with the right and left legs two times more.

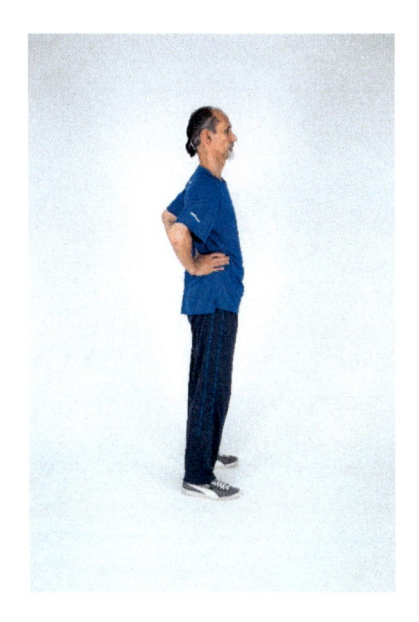

Fig. 14.1

Figs. 14.2 and 14.3

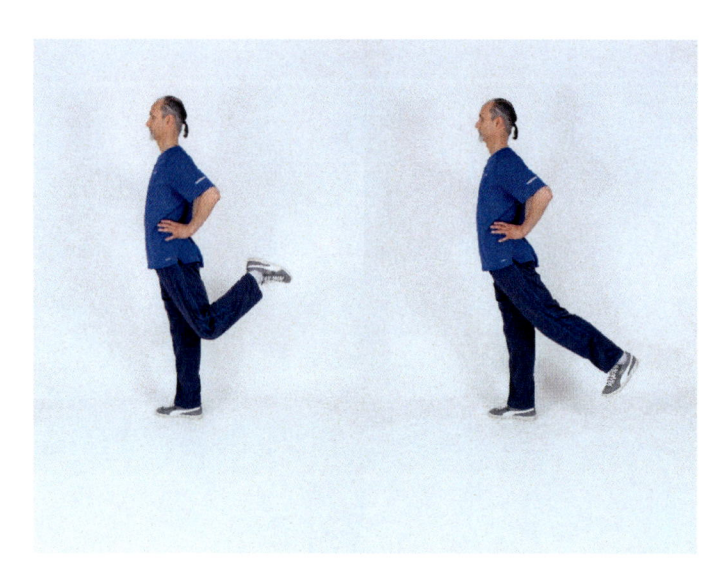

Figs. 14.4 and 14.5

Common mistakes

- ➢ Not stabilizing the pelvis.
- ➢ Thrusting the pelvis forward.
- ➢ Leaning forward.
- ➢ Raising the knee.
- ➢ Rotating the foot in or out excessively.

Main benefits

- Releases muscle tightness from the lower back.
- Helps tone up and strengthen the buttocks and lower back muscles.
- Stimulates the acupuncture point Urinary Bladder #40 on the posterior crease of the knee, which helps releasing tightness from the sacrum and lower spine areas.
- Helps strengthening the hamstrings muscle group.

15. EXTENDING AND FLEXING THE BACK

Description of the exercise

1. Stand with the feet together.

2. Place the hands on the lower back with the palms supporting the lumbar spine (Figs. 15.1 and 15.2).

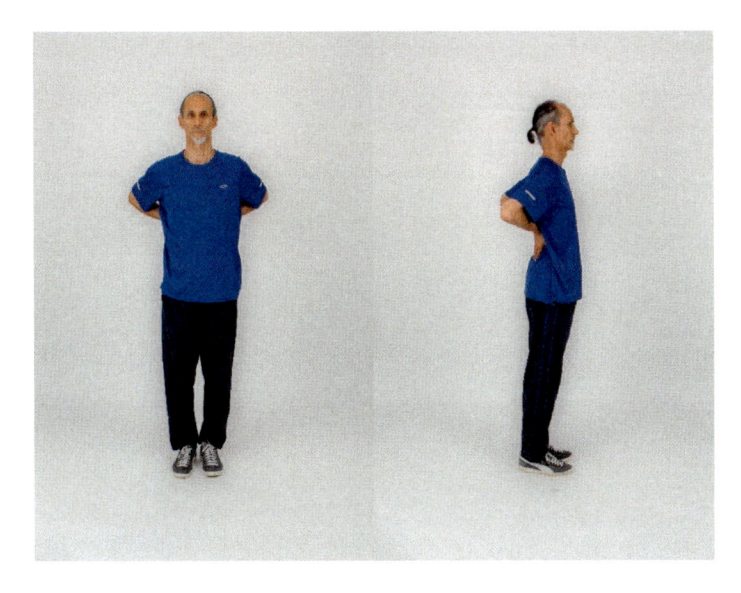

Figs. 15.1 and 15.2

3. Gently, push forward with the hands, extending or arching the lower back (Figs. 15.3 and 15.4).

4. Bend forward curving or bowing the back (Figs. 15.5 and 15.6).

Figs. 15.3 and 15.4

Figs. 15.5 and 15.6

5. When extending the back inhale and when flexing the back exhale.

6. Repeat extending and flexing the lower back several times.

Common mistakes

- ➢ Bending from the trunk instead of the waist.
- ➢ Arching the spine when bending forward.
- ➢ Insufficient flexing and extending from the lower back.
- ➢ Raising or lowering the head.
- ➢ Raising the shoulders.
- ➢ Twisting or turning the hips.

Main benefits

- Improves forward and backward mobility of the lower back region.
- Helps flexing and stretching the lower back.
- Increases flexibility of the lower back area.
- Helps strengthen and tone the lower back muscles.
- Relieves tightness and soreness from the lower back.

16. RESTING STANCE

Description of the exercise

1. Stand in a comfortable position with the feet shoulder-width apart, knees slightly bent, head upright, hips tucked, and lower back straight.

2. Bring the hands back over the waist area, resting the dorsum of the hands on the lower back (Figs. 16.1, 16.2, and 16.3).

3. Hold the stance for about five minutes or longer in a comfortable manner, making sure to keep the hips tucked, back straight, and lower back relaxed.

4. End the exercise bringing the hands to the lower abdomen.

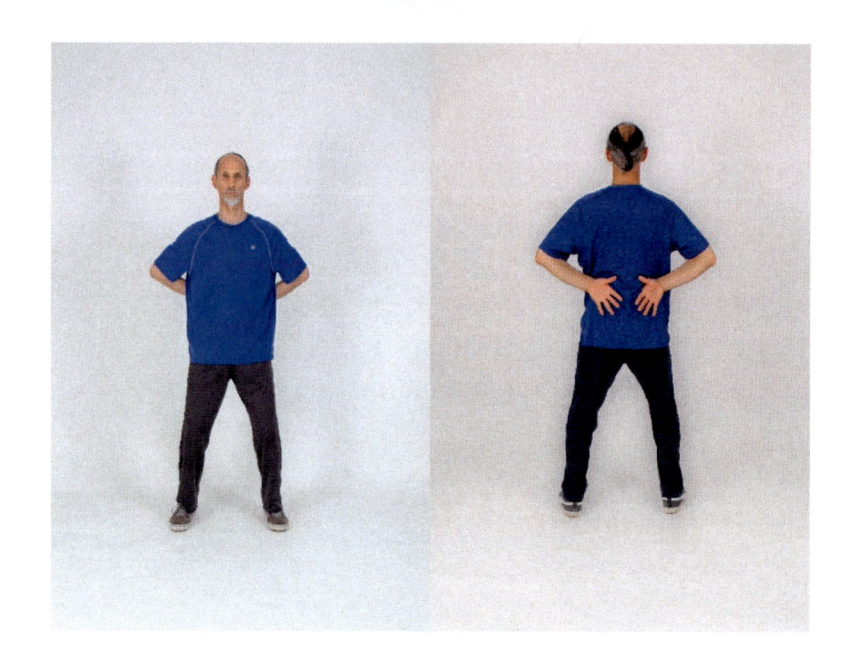

Figs. 16.1 and 16.2

Fig. 16.3

Common mistakes

- ➢ Arching the lower back.
- ➢ Raising the shoulders.
- ➢ Thrusting the chest.
- ➢ Pulling the elbows back and squeezing the shoulder blades.
- ➢ Thrusting the pelvis forward.

Main benefits

- Promotes the flow of vital energy and blood circulation to the lower back region.
- Helps energizing the lower back area, kidneys, and reproductive organs.
- Strengthens the kidneys and the original energy of the body (prenatal chi).
- Provides a resting and restorative effect upon the body and mind.
- Stimulates the descending movement of vital energy (chi) from the lungs thus improving breathing.

17. MASSAGING VITAL ENERGY POINTS

Description of the exercise

1. Stand with the feet at shoulder-width, knees slightly bent, and lower back straight.

2. Make loose fists and bring the hands back, resting the dorsum of the hands over the lower back area (fig. 17.1).

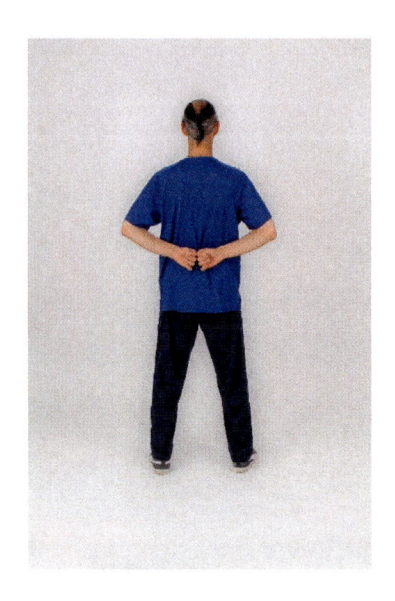

Fig. 17.1

3. Make circular rotations upward and inward toward the spine, massaging the lower back area (Figs. 17.2, 17.3, and 17.4).

4. Rotate the hands over the lower back area 50 times.

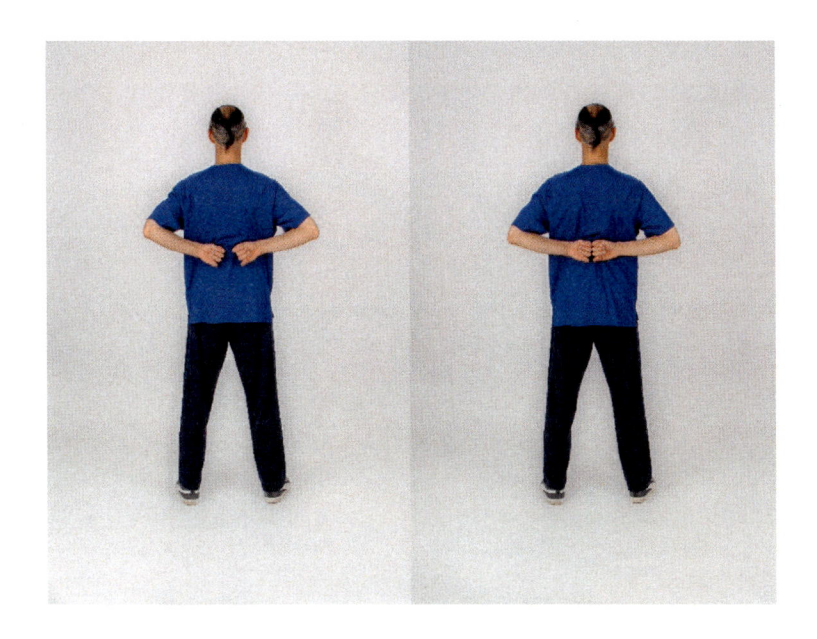

Figs. 17.2 and 17.3

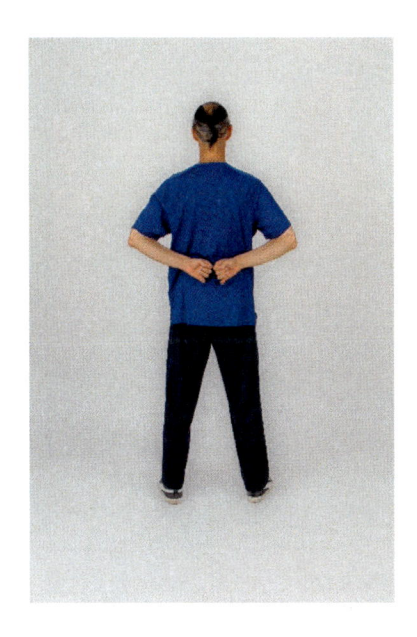

Fig. 17.4

5. With the dorsum of the hands, rub up and down the lower back area 25 times (Figs. 17.5 and 17.6).

6. Rub the sacrum area up and down 25 times (Fig. 17.7).

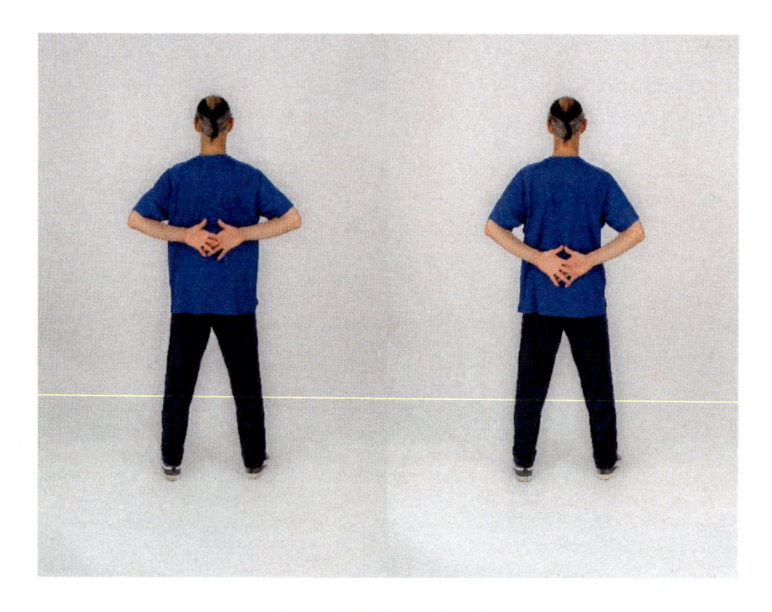

Figs. 17.5 and 17.6

Fig. 17.7

7. Making loose fists, gently pat the lower back area alternating the hands 25 times (Fig. 17.8).

8. Pat the sacrum area with loose fists alternating the hands 25 times (Figs. 17.9 and 17.10).

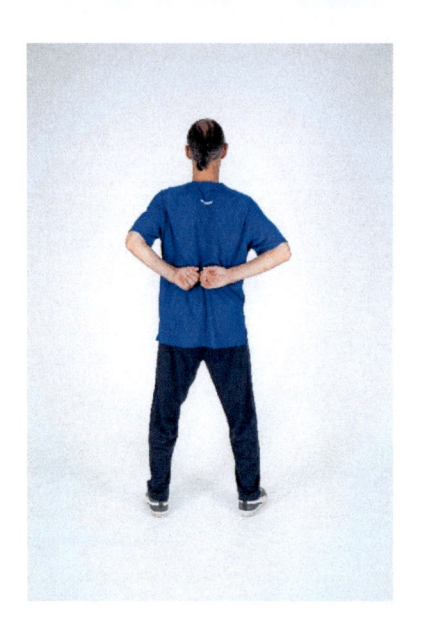

Fig. 17.8

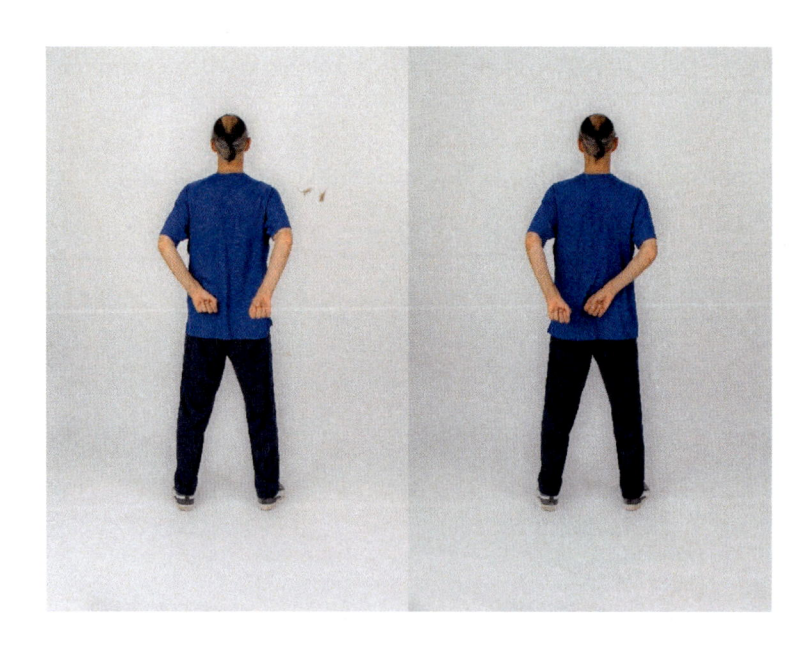

Figs. 17.9 and 17.10

9. With the back of the hands or loose fists, pat the lateral aspect of the buttocks 25 times (Figs. 17.11 and 17.12).

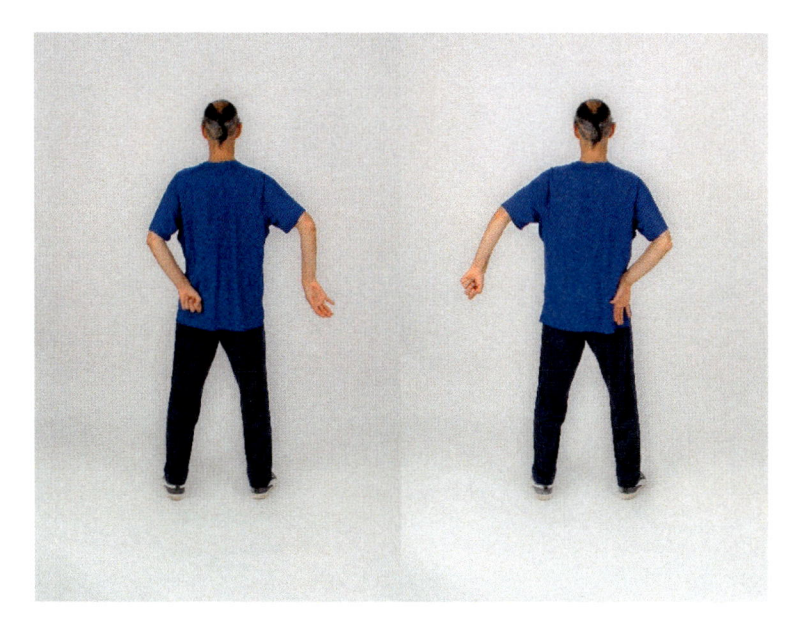

Figs. 17.11 and 17.12

10. With loose fists pat the hips 25 times (Figs. 17.13 and 17.14).

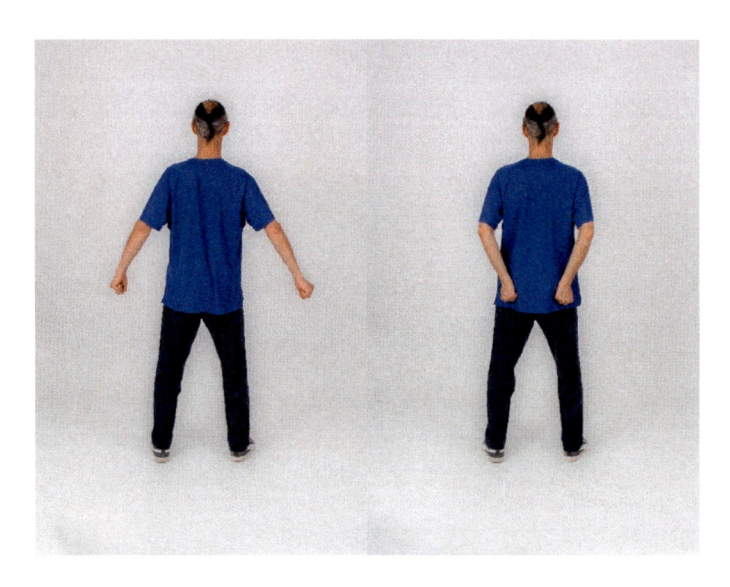

Figs. 17.13 and 17.14

11. With loose fists pat the lower calf muscle 10 times (Figs. 17.15 and 17.16).

Figs. 17.15 and 17.16

12. End bringing the hands to the lower abdomen.

Observations

1. One also can rub the lower back area up and down with the palms.

2. When patting the lower back area do it gently.

Common mistakes

- ➢ Raising the shoulders.
- ➢ Arching the lower back.
- ➢ Patting either too strongly or too loosely.

Main benefits

- Stimulates energy flow and blood circulation to the lower back and the hips.
- Helps to loosen up the waist and lower back muscles.

- Strengthens the kidney functions.
- Alleviates tightness, stiffness, and pain of the lower back.
- Helps preventing and relieving chronic lower back muscle strain.
- Relieves tightness of the buttocks and the hips region.
- Improves circulation to the lower extremities.
- Relieves tightness of the calf muscle.
- Stimulates the return of venous blood from the lower extremities back to the lungs and heart.
- Alleviates tiredness and aching of the legs.
- Relieves reproductive disorders such as painful or difficult menses, infertility, low sex drive, impotence, and weak and dribbling urination.
- Stimulates 'the second heart' area on the calf muscle thus promoting energy flow and blood circulation.

Precautions and contraindications

- Patting over the lower back area and the kidneys is contraindicated in cases of severe kidney disease.
- This exercise is contraindicated in cases of lower back pain caused by tumors, fracture, or tuberculosis.
- Do not perform this exercise during acute infections, fever, or colds.

18. MASSAGING THE EARS

Description of the exercise

1. This exercise can be practiced standing or sitting.

2. Take hold of the ears with the hands, placing the index finger on the front and the thumb on the back of the ear. The other three fingers are held folded on the palm (Figs. 18.1 and 18.2).

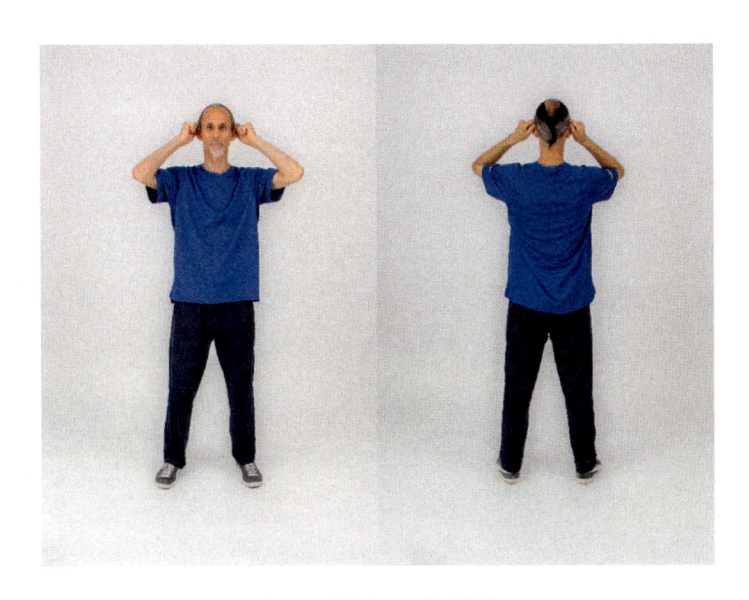

Figs. 18.1 and 18.2

3. Press and massage the ears from the top downwards, until the ears get warm (Figs. 18.3 and 18.4,).

4. Then, gently pull the ears down from top to bottom three times (Figs. 18.5, 18.6, 18.7, and 18.8).

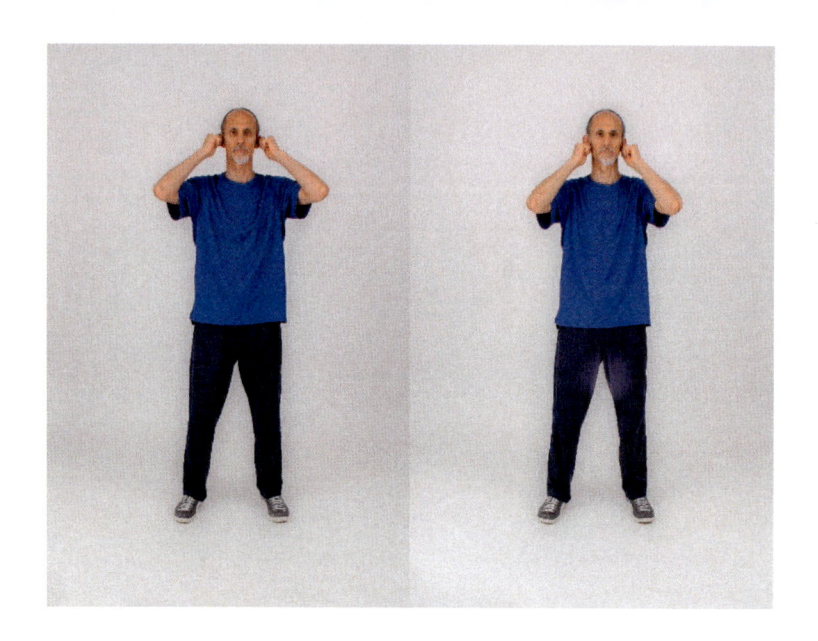

Figs.18.3 and 18.4

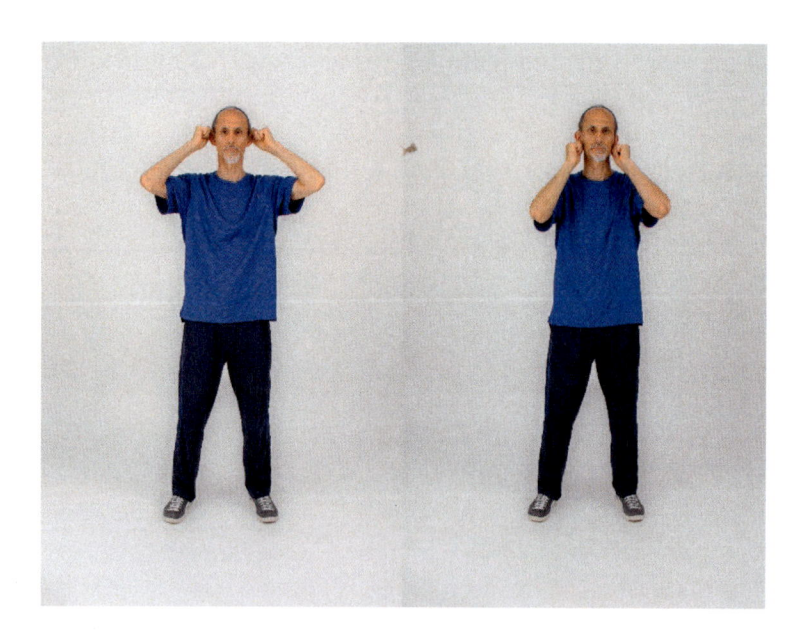

Figs. 18.5 and 18.6

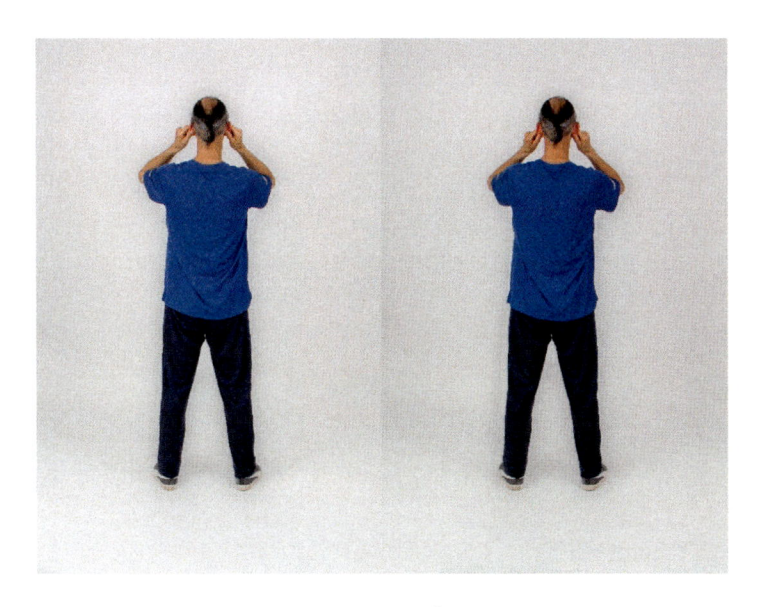

Figs. 18.7 and 18.8

5. End the exercise bringing the hands to the lower abdomen.

Common mistakes

- ➢ Raising the shoulders.
- ➢ Pressing and massaging the ears either too lightly or too heavily.

Main benefits

- Promotes energy flow and blood circulation throughout the body.
- Helps warming the body.
- Stimulates the kidneys.
- Benefits the lower back.
- Calms and soothes the mind.
- Helps to relieve and prevent hearing disorders like tinnitus and poor hearing.

###

Thank you for reading this book. It is my motivation that you benefited from following and practicing the Qigong exercises presented in this book. If you enjoyed, can you please take a moment to leave me a review at your favorite retailer?

Camilo Sanchez, L. Ac, MAOM

About the author

Camilo Sanchez, L. Ac, MAOM

With thirty years of clinical and teaching experience in acupuncture and Chinese medicine, Camilo has shared his life-long passion of the Oriental healing arts with thousands of clients throughout the United States and South America. Mr. Sanchez is a licensed acupuncturist with a master's degree in

Oriental medicine, published author, and recognized teacher of Qigong, Tai Chi, and Taoist Yoga.

Camilo Sanchez has an innate ability to integrate the best practices from the millenary wisdom of Oriental medicine with the latest integrative functional approaches to wellness. Camilo has guided thousands of individuals how to overcome chronic health challenges, experience sustainable levels of wellness, and tap into the innate ability of the body to heal.

Mr. Sanchez is past faculty member of the Acupuncture and Massage College in Miami, FL, and the Atlantic University of Chinese Medicine in Mars Hill, NC. He is founder and director of the Empower Life Center in Charlotte, North Carolina, where he provides customized treatment programs of acupuncture and Chinese medicine, metabolic balancing, integrated health, and authentic instruction of Tai Chi, Qigong, and Taoist yoga.

Camilo Sanchez can be reached for treatment programs, private instruction, mind and body wellness consulting, Qigong mentorship, speaking engagements, and corporate wellness at the Empower Life Center in Charlotte, NC.

Other titles by Camilo Sanchez

Daoist Meridian Yoga: Activating the Twelve Pathways for Energy Balance and Healing

Up-coming titles

Self-Healing with Qigong for Neck and Shoulders Pain

Self-Healing with Qigong for Digestive Disorders

Body of the Inner Elixir: A Comprehensive Guide to Taoist Qigong

Connect with Camilo Sanchez

Follow me on Twitter: twitter: @ElixirQigong

Friend me on Facebook: facebook/empowerlifecenter

Empower Life Center
14136 Lancaster Hwy
Pineville, NC 28134
704-542-8088
info@empowerlifecenter.com
http://www.empowerlifecenter.com

Made in the USA
Las Vegas, NV
14 November 2021